Letters from Grandpa

a primer for life

by Gene Kesselman

foreword and edited by Scott Kesselman

Library of Congress Control Number:
2017900601

ISBN: 978-0997986709

Cover design by Victoria Bottlick

This book is dedicated to Bill Kesselman, my son and the father of my grandchildren, Adam, Steven and Scott. Its existence would not have been possible without his devotion to our family and its heritage, resulting in the preservation of these letters for future generations.

CONTENTS

INTRODUCTION

THE LETTERS

Foreword

I have never met anyone who grabs life more than my Grandpa. He is always seeking out someone to talk to, making the most of each day, constantly learning as the wisest man you will ever meet and every moment becoming wiser. He can never pass up a moment to brighten someone's day with honest and thoughtful observations, a gentle smile and his sincere good wishes.

With these letters my grandpa has created a valuable legacy. So far he has chronicled over 90 years — memorable encounters and the challenges of life and of a nation from World War II to the Sept. 11th and the war on terror. It includes all his greatest lessons from a lifetime of travel and discourse. From his first radio to his first PC and now his first iPad, Grandpa Gene's letters burst with life and offer ageless wisdom amid the constantly changing world around us.

Every letter in this collection on its own can change your life — perhaps reinforcing an old perspective or revealing flaws in human habit with one-of-a-kind observations. Together these letters stand as the wisdom of a century, a great philosophical work arising from a nation's commitment to freedom and liberty, and a passionate love of language and correspondence between a caring grandpa and his grandchildren.

My Grandpa began writing regularly to us when I was 10

years old, right around the start of the new millennium. When my 8-year-old brother and I started reading the letters, we had little idea the valuable lessons contained in each one. Over a decade and a half of receiving letters and reading them over, it becomes apparent how carefully crafted each letter is and how my grandpa's experiences and his brilliant way of conveying them through the written word have prepared me for life. Life is full of struggle and hardship, and this is true for every single one of us. It makes conversation our greatest asset — learning from other people, because we are all in it the same.

My grandpa has taught me to greet each morning with an open mind, to share my ideas and to listen and absorb others', and to always stay active, following my heart. The following pages are more than just structured words, they create an accessible foundation for living a happy and successful life.

Scott Kesselman
East Orange, New Jersey
June 2013

Preface For Adults

The process of writing a book has never appealed to me, but letters have, and I have written over 70. Fortunately, they did become a book — this book — and all the letters that fill it are from and mostly to my grandchildren.

As I was approaching my 80th year I began thinking of my life — the failures, the mistakes and the bad choices — and the counter — more good choices, the many happy results and the very many successes. Life is all this and more.

I began to realize that my long years were one extended and continuous learning process in which I gained confidence, experience, insight and certainly greater wisdom. We, the older generation, truly know the route better, with more knowledge of how to negotiate the twists and turns. We can more clearly understand and even foresee the possible results of cause and effect.

All that hard-earned wisdom would eventually be lost unless I passed on my personal and family history to my children and grandchildren. My heritage belongs to them — only my life is mine alone. I owe them by virtue of their birth the story of their family, the America I witnessed before they were born, and its impact on my life and times. The lessons of my journey can help make their voyage more productive and more successful.

But how do you pass your heritage onto your family and, particularly, your children and grandchildren? There are many ways; you can utilize the written word, digital recording, video recording or one-on-one conversation. You have to at least pick one, and you have to tell the truth, even the unflattering truth.

We all make mistakes, bad choices, do and say things we often regret. The only way you can be convincing and believable to your family is to be honest. Only then can they learn from both your pitfalls and your successes and be able to add your benefits to their growing maturity.

I suggest that you first peruse this book. Absorb its purpose, and then start to read it, usually one or two letters at a time. Kindly allow some workable ideas to germinate in your mind, and then relate them to your own life. Think back to long forgotten years, and continue this effort until you are ready to begin communicating your story to your own children and grandchildren.

It is never too late or too early in their lives for you to begin offering them your personal story and their heritage. It will give your family, children and grandchildren a greater understanding and appreciation for not only who you are, but for what you are. They will love you even more. Just do it!

I chose the medium of email letters. They can be saved and reread many times and eventually become available to their children and grandchildren. Can you imagine the surprise and joy of your descendants receiving letters from their great-grandparents?

My letters in this book follow one of three distinct themes: America 80 years ago, my own life and times, and finally ideas to assist in personal development and behavior. The first group allows my grandchildren to understand and appreciate the very different America in which I grew up. The second group tells them who I was and how I came to be who I am today, including personal and outside factors that influenced me and my journey. The last group makes them aware of important personality traits, communication skills and mind-set that will facilitate all their endeavors.

Why do all this? Why bother? Let us start with this premise. All grandchildren love their grandparents. It's a given. But they still think of them as the old folks. Whatever your age, that is all they see. Compared to them, you are old. If you are retired, you have no job, you have money, you travel and you have plenty of spare time. They love you, sure, but they don't really know you or know your long history. They only know what they see. They don't realize that you were young once, with the same growing problems and youthful uncertainties that they are experiencing.

You should realize that they need your heritage and the opportunity to benefit from your accumulated experience and hard-earned wisdom. It has taken you a lifetime to acquire and is unique to you. You would be giving your grandchildren something much more important than your acquired assets, which they can never lose, sell, spend or have stolen.

They will then begin to understand the long road you have traveled and be able to reap important benefits from the lessons of your life. This labor of love is cost free — no long lawyer conferences, no wills, trusts, trustees or legal fees. You are giving them your years and giving your years added purpose. Think of it this way: Your life belongs to you, but your heritage belongs to your children and grandchildren.

P.S. — If you want some corroboration of the effectiveness of this effort on my family, kindly read the letters from my grandchildren to me. It is all the thanks I could ever wish for.

Gene Kesselman
West Caldwell, New Jersey
May 2016

Preface  For Young People

The letters in this book were originally written for my grandchildren to tell them a story — a story in brief of my long life and all that I have learned over the years. I wanted them to know more about me than just the old man they see. To them, it may seem that I have been old all my life. How can they possibly visualize what I must have been like as a young man unless I tell them?

However, there is another purpose to this book that can greatly benefit you, as well as my grandchildren. Let me explain. We, the seniors, lived through and beyond our young years a long time ago. Our journey was an older version of your current journey, different in some respects, but no less dramatic. Our problems are the same: find out who we truly are, adapt our innate abilities to life's needs and find our place in the world. We have been there. We know.

Except for the letters that talk about my time growing up in America from the 1920s, most of them could have been written just as well by your father or grandfather. From a long life, we have learned a great deal about what mostly works or doesn't work. In most of the letters I tell you about personality and behavioral traits that are conducive to successful outcomes. I tell you about procedures that smooth potential bumps and clear the debris in the road — tools that can save you time (sometimes years) and, of course, money. All this is gleaned from my personal experience.

This is certainly not a how-to book in any sense. It is just common sense, general in nature, and requires an open and flexible mind. All of life is a learning process — learning how to live, how to prosper, how to stay healthy, and how to get along with your fellow man and gain their respect. Don't delay making necessary and thoughtful decisions, and follow through on everything you do. Be honest, honest with yourself and with others. It's your life and your results. Good luck in all your endeavors.

Gene Kesselman
West Caldwell, New Jersey
May 2016

The Letters

Simplicity in a Complex World

February 21, 2000

Dear Scott and Steven,

Most people like things to be simple. It makes it easier to
think and to make timely decisions. Simplicity is a worthwhile
goal, but it is difficult to attain in this day and age. Very little
today is simple. We have too many impressions of an intrusive
world impinging on our minds. There is the constant pressure
of pervasive advertising targeting us from every direction that
we cannot escape. It tells us what to buy, what to eat, where to go
and how to live our lives.

There are computers, high-definition TVs, DVDs, cell phones,
iPods, iPads and personal electronic gadgets of every description
that put the world at our fingertips. We can fly anywhere on
the globe in just hours — London overnight, Australia in a day.
The superhighway system makes our country a playground
of destinations. The GPS lets us know exactly where we are
located. The internet makes information and communications fast
and inexpensive commodities.

We are confronted daily, even hourly, with countless choices
as to how to spend our time. Do we go the movies, watch
television, go on the internet, book a flight or cruise to anywhere
worldwide, attend a concert, play a video game, do homework,

and on and on? Life today can be very complicated. So let us compare modern day America to that simpler time when I was a boy of 13.

A good vacation was a two-hour auto ride away in the Catskill Mountains, which was loaded with hotels, or perhaps Atlantic City. Mount Freedom, near Morristown, with about 25 hotels, and West Orange, with three hotels, all on Pleasant Valley Way, were considered vacation spots in the country, particularly by New Yorkers. Back then they thought New Jersey was the Far West and the Hudson River was the Mississippi. Only the rich could afford to go to Europe or some other distant land, mainly by boat. Europe was a five- to seven-day trip ocean crossing one-way. Asia by boat was a 14- to 20-day voyage. How much time could you spend sightseeing if just getting there took so long? A European vacation required at least a month or more.

Trains and intercity buses were the choices between cities in the United States. A train trip to Los Angeles from New York took almost a week. Niagara Falls, New York, a favorite for honeymooners, was an overnight train ride. Plane travel was in its infancy and expensive. Propeller-driven planes were very noisy, flew at half the speed of jets and less than half the distance before landing to refuel. A plane flight to Los Angeles from New York took 10 hours. Flying to Europe took two refueling stops, at Gander, Newfoundland, and Shannon, Ireland. Growing up in North Jersey, far away for us was Pittsburgh or Buffalo at 400 miles. No one could even dream about vacationing far from home. It could be costly and time consuming, and money and spare time were rare in the depression days before World War II.

In the home there was only the radio or a wind-up phonograph for entertainment. There was a single telephone attached to the wall in only one room. When it rang, you had to go to it. Most phones had two to four families using the same line. If you were lucky to even own a car, there was only one in the family. Whoever had the most important need got to use it. Two-car families were few and rich. Women drivers were rare. My mother and my friends' mothers never drove a car. Children old enough to drive had to ask well in advance to use the family car, and not too often. Sundays we went for the regular weekly car ride for an hour or so, then back home for supper.

Eating out was almost unthinkable. Fast food restaurants were unknown and highways were few. Centrally located streets were extended to the next town. Families usually did most social things together. Friends visited friends in their homes. The father took the car to work and the mother, if she had to go anywhere, took a bus or trolley. Nights out were mostly spent at the homes of friends. Movies and dinner out was not a common option. We had company, and they had company. Everyone took turns having the group over for dinner or cards and a late evening snack.

Daily newspapers gave us the news. There were separate editions for morning, noon and evening in order to try to be current. If something big happened in the world, a so-called extra was printed and hawked on street corners by paperboys. In Newark and other cities there were newsreel theaters that only showed motion pictures of two week or older news. The show took about an hour, and people went just to get a brief and outdated look at what was happening in the world.

At the movies, in addition to the previews, they would show a five-minute recap of news that by today's standards was old. News film had to be flown back from wherever it was taken and then chemically processed, and that was time consuming. There were no correspondents traveling the world and reporting back live, even on radio.

Downtown was the big shopping, movie and dining area. Most buses and trolleys went to and through downtown from every direction. Remember, there were no malls or shopping centers. First-run movies were shown downtown first and then weeks later in theaters in all the outlying neighborhoods of the city. The movies consisted of a single screen and one audience. All the big department stores and good restaurants were downtown, and they prospered. That's where the all action was and where we took our girlfriends on dates, mostly by bus or trolley. In a sense our lives were strictly local, confined to the immediate neighborhoods in which we lived and downtown.

After World War II things began to change rapidly. Fifteen million returning servicemen required cars, homes and jobs. Others, like me, wanted to finish their education. The whole country had been mobilized into one big war machine. Industry had to switch literally overnight from war to civilian production. There were shortages in some commodities for years, including automobiles. The first television sets came out in the late '40s. They were nine inches, black and white, and very expensive. Whoever could afford to buy one had many visitors coming over to watch. Ten people, more or less, would often squeeze in front of a little set, gawking at a poor picture with squeaky sound. I watched a couple of World Series at a neighbor's house. When he wanted to go to bed or just stop watching, I had to go home and listen on the radio.

As you can see, America was far different in the 1930s than it is today. Seventy years is a long time in the affairs of men and nations. Picture the changes in the United States from the Revolutionary War to the Civil War, then from the Civil War to World War I. Even if I could, I would not want to go back to the days of my youth, and for what purpose? The world is not the same as it was and neither am I. I have seen a great deal, and I have done a great deal. We must move on to new challenges to remain vital. Those early years can be vividly recreated only in my memory as I lived it. To paraphrase the title of a book by Thomas Wolfe, you can't go home again. Home just isn't there anymore.

As the two of you grow up and travel the world, you will realize that you have to make your own discoveries. The lessons of history and the wisdom of our fathers are difficult to transmit. You must experience life for yourselves as individuals and create your own memories. Only then will your lessons be truly learned and become part of who you are. Good luck in all your endeavors.

Grandma Myra and I love you both very much.

Grandpa Gene

Home

March 18, 2000

Dear Scott, Steven, Raellen and Billy,

Our winter in Florida is slowly coming to an end. Your visit
will cap a busy season. Yet Grandma and I will be glad to return
home. Spring and fall in New Jersey are the most beautiful times
of the year. Florida is one-dimensional, warm and hot. It is time
to leave here. Also, we will be able to see you more often. Friends
are fine to have, and I know you have many, but there is no group
of people stronger than family, and you are our family. That alone
makes New Jersey our real home.

   Years ago, when I was in the U.S. Air Force, I served in
Louisiana, New Mexico, the Philippine islands and other places
for a total of three years. I used to dream of home. No matter
where you travel or live, there is one place you can call home.
Of course, everyone in the armed forces was away from home,
and all of us used to wait anxiously for letters and packages from
home. We would have to wait for hours, even days, to use the two
pay phones on the base, just to hear the voices of my father and
mother. Note that there were thousands of men on the base and
only two phones!

   There are many things we remember as we grow up. That
is one reason I take lots of pictures. It helps me to remember,
and all of us can enjoy the memories years later. Let me quote

something I read somewhere: "You must live a good, honorable, productive life. Then, when you get older and think back, you will be able to enjoy it a second time."

Happy memories. Grandma and I love all of you. See you soon.

Grandpa

Spring

April 9, 2000

Dear Scott, Steven, Raellen and Billy,

Spring is here, and with it a new beginning for Mother Earth. The growing season has begun, and soon there will be color all around us from flowers, bushes, trees and grass. Later, fresh vegetables and fruit, tomatoes, peaches, apples will burst with life from vines and trees. The days are longer and the weather mild and warm, and we begin to do all the warm weather things.

Every season has its pleasures, and we learn to adapt our lives to the changing scenes of the year. Now it is golf and tennis, baseball and soccer. We do the things we enjoy that keep us occupied and happy, both outside the house and inside. You should also make time for reading and talking with other people. Every experience, every happening, is a learning one. We can even learn from our mistakes. There is a lesson for the future in everything we do, if you can find it. These lessons teach us to modify and improve our behavior as we grow up, to become a better person, wiser in our thinking, better students in school, more tolerant and understanding of other people and the world we live in.

Happiness as a person really comes from within ourselves, when we always do the best we can, in school, in the home and outside. Always strive to improve, to do better than before. Trying your best in everything you do will make you happy — happy with yourselves, your friends and your family. We love all of you.

Grandma and Grandpa

Vacation

April 14, 2000

Dear Steven, Scott, Raellen and Billy,

Soon, all of you will be here in Florida on vacation. Vacations are wonderful times in our lives. Let us consider them a reward for the times that you are not on vacation. You may then ask what I mean by that — not on vacation. Well, when you're not on vacation, you are supposed to be doing your job, which is different at different ages. Your job is different than Daddy's, or Uncle David's, or Grandma and Grandpa's.

Your primary job now, among other things, is to go to school and learn all you can. You also have other jobs that are equally important. At your age you should be learning good habits of work, like doing your homework well and on time — really doing everything that is your responsibility well and on time. Then people will say that Steven and Scott are dependable, that you can always count on them to do the right thing.

You should be developing good personal habits, like developing a good diet — not only what you like, but what you know is good for you. Also very important is to be a good person: honest, truthful, cooperative, understanding and helpful to others. These are only a few of the many jobs you have as you grow up to be happy, healthy adults. Grandma and I know that you are doing all of the above good things and much more, and we are very proud of both of you. If we could pick two of the best boys and best grandchildren in the whole world, it is no contest. We would proudly pick Steven and Scott. Grandma and I love you both very much.

Grandpa

Mistakes and Decisions

April 29, 2000

Dear Steven, Scott, Raellen and Billy,

Your vacation with us has come and gone, but we have happy memories of being together, living together and doing things together. These times and all other events and things we do daily, when strung together over the years, make up the fabric of our lives. We add to that fabric every day, by what we learn, how we conduct ourselves, what we do and the decisions we make about everything.

All of us, at every age, make decisions: me, Daddy, Raellen, Uncle David and both of you. The trick is to make wise decisions that are good for you and those you love. You see, the more you learn, and the more knowledge you have, the wiser you can be. When you are young, many important decisions are made for you by your parents and others in charge of your growing up, like teachers.

As you grow older, and I hope wiser, you will be making more and more of your own decisions that will determine what kind of person you are, how you will do things, where and when you will go places. These will include who will be your friends, what you will wear, how you will conduct yourselves in private and in public places.

Not all of your decisions will turn out to be good ones, and remember, all of us, everyone has the same problems, and sometimes we make mistakes. We try to correct the ones that don't turn out well, and we try to learn some lessons from our mistakes. Making mistakes is normal for everyone. That's how people who are smart become wise, by making mistakes, learning from them, and trying to make wiser decisions next time.

Smart and wise are two different things. Smart means knowing a lot of information. Wisdom is using that information to benefit yourselves and those you love. In other words, make the best and wisest decisions you can based on good knowledge and information. So you see, becoming wiser takes time and more growing up. Grandma and I are proud of both of you, and we know you will use these words from Grandpa wisely. See you soon.

Grandma and I love you very much.

Grandpa

A Walk

October 8, 2000

Dear boys,

I took a walk this afternoon. It was not an ordinary walk but a special one. It was a fall walk. This morning I played tennis for over an hour and didn't plan to do any more exercise today. After lunch, I rested, read a little, watched some television and then looked out the window. The sun was bright, casting long shadows. The clouds were full and fluffy, sailing slowly across the sky. So I put on a jacket and cap and my sunglasses, which I never go without, and stepped out into this paradise.

No camera is really good enough to capture this picture. It will only let you see it, but not feel it: the coolness of the air on your skin and the long shadows delineating every living bush and tree. It takes an appreciative mind and heart to enjoy this free and beautiful scene. I know that both of you have that kind of understanding mind and heart. Very few people or cars moved; the place seemed almost deserted. So I took a walk.

Fall is my favorite time of the year. It is not summer, and it is not winter. What I mean to say is that it is not extreme. More often it is pleasant. It takes the best of both and blends them into a feast for the soul.

What do I do when I walk?

Well, I look and listen. Nature talks, you know — the rustle of leaves, the moan of wind passing your ears, the happy song of a bird, the bubble of water rushing over rocks. I never take a radio with me. It would interfere with my thoughts. Yes, I think when I walk. I think how lucky I am to have two great-grandchildren, whom we love very much. I think how lucky I am just to be alive and able to enjoy the blessings of nature, my family and friends. Those are the important things.

We are not alone on this Earth. We are all one big family, and we should always try to make life pleasant and enjoyable for ourselves and others. If you give joy and peace, you receive joy and peace. Nature teaches us that. Feed and water a tree, and it will grow.

Yet sometimes nature is not pleasant, and we don't like that. There's a thunderstorm, a hurricane, a blizzard. Life is like that also. Things happen that we don't like and maybe don't understand. But as sure as day follows night every day, if we always do our best, do the right thing, work hard and keep learning new things every day, in time, the sun will shine. Remember, it is always shining somewhere on this earth.

So I walk — for fun, for exercise, to clear my mind and think, to enjoy nature and the world around me. You don't have to always walk alone. You can walk with your brother, your dad, a friend or anyone. You can talk or be quiet, walk fast or slow, think of everything or nothing. Every walk is a joy. Tomorrow, I will arise, have breakfast and take a walk. I can't wait for a new day to begin.

We love you, always,
Grandma and Grandpa

Scott's 11th Birthday

November 18, 2000

Dear Scott,

You will find as you grow up that every age offers something special. They offer you opportunities as well as challenges. How you meet them defines you as a boy and later as a man.

As you celebrate your 11th birthday, Grandma Myra and I are very proud of you as a person, not only with exceptional mental abilities but with wonderful human qualities as well. By mental qualities I mean you are bright, learn quickly and you are well aware of what is happening in the world around you. Your human qualities include an engaging personality, a pleasant disposition and a kindness towards others. You like people, and they like you. In many ways, you are already very grown up but with the charm and wonderment of youth. You are one of those rare people that it is nice to be around.

You make people you meet feel good about themselves. You know how to listen, because you know that when you listen, you learn. Many times you say things that are wise beyond your years. So as you celebrate your 11th birthday, Grandma Myra and I wish you good health, happiness and much success in everything you do. We love you.

Grandpa Gene

To Steven: On the Occasion of Scott's 11th Birthday

November 18, 2000

Dear Steven,

Everything that I wrote to Scott can be written for you also. Perhaps that is why you are not only brothers but also good friends. I like the way you talk to each other, just like adults. You discuss the affairs of the day, you look out for and help one another in whatever you may be doing at the time. You share things, both material and otherwise, particularly a wonderful sense of humor.

Yet, you are both different in many ways. You are individuals, each with his own personality and temperament. That is the way God intended. Steven, Grandma Myra and I are very proud of you. To us you were never a little boy, but a young adult. You are wise beyond your years, and you understand the real meaning of words and ideas.

You and Scott are lucky to have each other, to grow up together, and become fine and productive human beings. As I wrote to Scott, Grandma Myra and I wish you good health, happiness and much success in everything you do. We love you.

Grandpa Gene

Family and Judaism

January 11, 2001

Dear Steven and Scott,

It looks like Grandma Myra and I will be leaving for Florida very soon. It is later than we usually go, but we had to clear up some medical problems. All is well now, but it is always sad, because we will miss both of you very much, as well as Raellen and your Dad and Uncle David. We enjoy the time we spend with you for many reasons. You are good company, you are pleasant and bright, and we talk about many things.

When the weather is nice, we go outside and explore and enjoy our surroundings. We love being with you and doing things together. Sometimes you have friends that are all of these things, and friends are always an important part of our lives. Yet, when you are family, it makes it even better. Family ties should be strong. It means a continuity of life, a passing on of heritage, history, knowledge, learning and wisdom.

You are our grandchildren, and we want you to benefit from all that we know, so that your lives can be more productive and happier. The Jewish people have the longest continuous history of any people on earth. Our calendar goes back over 5,000 years, beyond recorded history. Many major religions on earth stem from the Jews, who were the first people on earth to believe in one God. That was a major breakthrough in human thought so long ago.

Jews wrote the Old Testament, the first bible, on which all the later ones are based. Why have the Jews lasted so long? Why are there Jews who live in countries that enjoy free speech so prominent in education, literature, music, the sciences, medicine, the arts, politics, business and commerce? Hundreds, even thousands of books have been written on this subject. Yet you and I can boil it down to a few sentences.

Jews believe in family as the basic foundation of society. We believe in education and learning. We know the difference between right and wrong, like the Ten Commandments. We believe in laws that govern the relationships between people, and we recognize the right of everyone to be free, to live his own life as he wishes as long as he doesn't trespass on the rights of others.

Jews, for millennia, have been the conscience of the world, and the world is a much better place for our having persisted and endured. Grandma Myra and I know that both of you will grow up to be worthy of your great heritage and carry it on into the new century. We love you very much.

Grandpa Gene

Moving

January 23, 2001

Dear Folks,

We arrived in Florida on Friday. Next time we fly and ship the car. However, it worked out this time, because we canceled our trip twice. The monitor came yesterday, Monday. I left it on the floor and had a maintenance man here heft it up to the desk today. As you can see, the computer is up and running. I connected everything properly. Thank all of you very much for the monitor. It is a pleasure to use and view and saves my eyes.

The weather is cool here. Anything under 60 is cold and precludes any wearing of shorts and stuff. But I take my walks — started yesterday with a mile and did a mile today. I haven't done much exercise in the last two months with the weather up North and my medical problems. All that is behind me now, I am fine. Soon I will be playing golf. Mother is also starting to walk in the morning.

Boys, even at almost 80 years of age, Grandpa still keeps busy and active in order to stay healthy and be able to do things. My older brother Uncle Sol says to keep moving, because it is hard to hit a moving target. That means he wants to stay healthy longer and live longer. He is anxious to see all of you when you come to Florida. We haven't seen him yet, because he is away visiting his family in Arizona. Soon, I will send you another letter. I have no idea what I will write. But I sit down at the computer and thoughts seem to come. It is easy to write to someone you love, and Grandma Myra and I love all of you very much.

Grandpa Gene

Air Force and Discipline

January 27, 2001

Dear Steven and Scott,

I want to tell you story about a 21-year-old boy who volunteered for service in the Air Force of the United States during World War II. He was a quiet boy, came from a nice family of loving parents with four boys. He was the youngest and very shy growing up with much older adults. He did all the normal things that all boys did in that time — street ball, street games including stick ball, football, hanging out at the local corner with his friends, public school, high school, began college and wondered what to do with his life. The war decided that for him. But rather than be called up in the general draft and possibly ending up as a foot soldier, he chose to enlist and determine his own destiny and service.

He picked the Air Force, passed all the tests including written, oral and psychological. He waited home for six long months until they had room at the classification center in Nashville, Tennessee. On March 24, 1943, he was uprooted from his comfortable home and family and thrust into a totally strange and rigid environment, like thousands of others.

He would never be alone anymore. He ate, slept, dressed and undressed, showered, toileted, exercised, waited in long lines for everything, even using the telephone and the bathroom, with hundreds of young men like him around all the time. There were more tests and questions, like how do you feel about the prospects of dying in aerial combat, or, if the situation arose, could you shoot and kill someone? This was not Route 10, or Randolph, New Jersey, anymore. Conditions were rough. He lived in a 100-foot-long, thin wooden barracks with 60 other boys in bunks, one above the other. It was heated inadequately with two coal stoves and had only one bathroom. When he awoke in the morning, his nose was stuffed with coal dust. He quickly dressed over his underwear, which he wore for two straight weeks at a time, and ran outside in the cold dark morning to stand roll call. Someday I will tell you more about this period. He passed all the tests and was classified for navigational training. The other two possibilities were pilot and bombardier. The navigator directs the course of the plane, or even the whole squadron if he is in the lead plane. In that case, they all follow his plane. The formation is easier to defend than one lone plane.

Between May and December 1943, this young man was reborn from a quiet, almost naive, totally inexperienced, untraveled, unworldly recruit into a 2nd Lieutenant Navigator flying officer in the United States Air Force. It involved strict discipline to rules and regulations, hard physical training, long periods of classroom instruction, tough exams and training flights all over the southeastern United States, from San Angelo, Texas, to Albany, Georgia, and over the Gulf of Mexico.

He once protected a fellow student in a flight lesson (there were three in our twin-engine A-7 trainers) from washing out the class by privately pointing out to him a serious error in his calculations that had us 200 miles south of where we actually were. He then fed the pilot the right information, and we were able to land at our training base, at Selman Field, Louisiana, in about 40 minutes instead of mistakenly thinking we were being hung out over the Gulf of Mexico with a lowering fuel supply and some confusion.

What lessons can you gather from this very foreshortened story that changed him and his life forever? He had learned to believe in himself — that he could persevere and do the job he knew he had to do, that he could adapt to almost any situation, that he must be responsible for his own actions, solve his own problems and blame no one else. He realized that he had the brains and the will and the discipline to realistically be anything he wanted to be and do anything he wanted to do.

All through the years, his enthusiasm for life has never waned. As his grandchildren, you have the same genes, the same opportunities to learn and grow, and become good solid responsible citizens. You will be called upon in your lifetime to do things that you think you cannot do. But remember your Grandpa, and find the discipline, the knowledge and the will. You have the brains and the energy to persevere and get the job done.

Grandma Myra and I love all of you very much.

Grandpa Gene

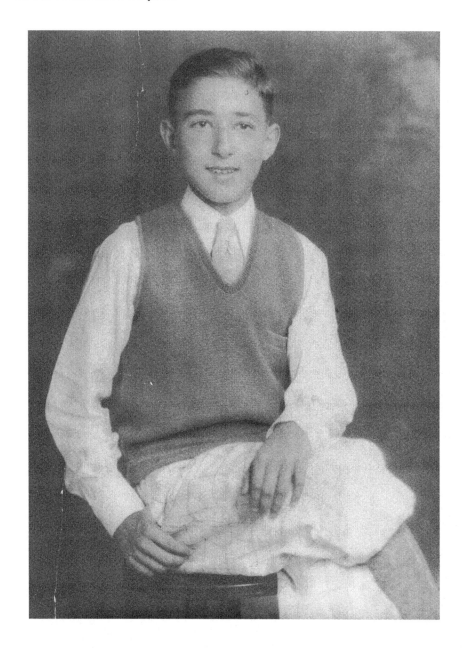

Grandpa Gene at age 12.

He later became a first lieutenent and navigator on a B-24 Bomber
in the U.S. Air Force.

The Unexpected

March 22, 2001

Dear Steven and Scott,

The calendar says that it is spring. If you were to look outside today, you will see that it is raining and cold, and it is anything but spring. It seems that nature does not always run according to plan. That's also true of life. Many things that we plan and attempt to do have a way of turning out differently than we expected. I'm sure that has happened to you any number of times. You have a game to play, but it rains. You are invited to a party, but you get sick and can't go. You may have a project for school or take a test, and the grades are not what you expected.

Even at your young ages, you are beginning to develop a philosophy of living, a way of looking at life and a way of handling both disappointment and success. To really be happy and enjoy life, you must be optimistic and positive about what you are doing, both in school and out. You must have faith in yourself, in your intelligence, in your honesty and goodness, and in your abilities. This may sound funny to you, but you must first like who you are in order for others to like you. You must respect yourself for your integrity and honesty, your ability to learn, and your desire to always do your best in every situation.

Now, that does not make you a better person than anyone else. It just means you are in a better position to be happier, to be more successful in your endeavors and to have lots of friends. When some things don't turn out the way you want them to, you have to adapt to new situations. You should take time to think and decide what to do next — do it, and move on. Don't concern yourself or waste time with things you cannot change, like the weather. Life is full of successes and disappointments, big or small. You must build upon your successes, and you must learn important lessons from your disappointments. Even success can often teach you something new. You are not alone.

These things happen to everyone — Daddy, me, all people. But always remember to keep trying and keep learning. Just as your body grows now, your mind can grow and learn all your life. That's how you gain wisdom. We love you, Raellen and Daddy very much, and we wish all of you good health and happiness.

Grandpa

Change, Father's Day 2001

June 17, 2001

Dear Steven and Scott,

I want to thank you for the very nice gift you gave me for
Father's Day. It has more wisdom than I have ever read in one
place. Let me qualify that for you. Wisdom can be read but
sometimes not understood. It depends on who is doing the
reading. Has he done enough, lived enough, learned enough,
understood enough, experienced enough to begin to know what
he is reading? Can he apply it to his everyday life, like going
to school, playing sports, meeting and talking to people, and
doing things that everyone does? Most important of all, can he
make wise decisions based on knowledge and good information?
Wisdom is the ability to think clearly, evaluate information,
imagine the consequences, make a decision, and then act.

Sometimes making a decision not to act is wise, because the
timing is not right, or a certain situation must first develop
before you do anything, or because you just don't have enough
information to make a wise decision. Even with all that, often the
decisions we do make do not turn out as we hoped or expected.

As humans, we can only do the best we can based on what we know at the time or what we expect other people to do or not do. We cannot control everything. In life situations change, and what is true one day may change the next day. Change should always be expected, and we have to learn to always be ready to adjust to new situations. That is the measure of being an adult and being wise. Wise people expect change — seasons change, climates change, people change as they grow and get older, even relationships between people change. Change is normal. It means growth, maturity, certainly variety and, more often, improvement. Expect change, understand it, embrace it and adjust comfortably to it.

I am proud of both of you, because I know you are wise, more than most young people your age. You are both good thinkers and thoughtful. You are both intelligent and quick learners. I know you can adjust to new situations and that you are comfortable with who you are. To me, you are young adults. Grandma and I are proud to be your grandparents. We love you both very much.

Grandpa Gene

P.S. – I am going to return the book to you in a few months, so that you can both refer to it often as you grow up. Learning is a lifelong occupation.

Steven's 10th Birthday

July 23, 2001

Dear Steven,

Congratulations and happy birthday from Grandma Myra and
Grandpa Gene! Your 10th birthday is a milestone in your life.
There will be many other milestones to celebrate. You can define
them either as birthdays, like your 20th, 25th, 30th, or occasions,
like your bar mitzvah at 13, your graduation from grade school
or high school or college. You can, if you want, make every day
an occasion to celebrate. Of course, you can't have a party every
day, but there are a lot of things you should appreciate all the
time. Let's see if we can find a few of them.

First, there are a lot of people who love you and a lot
of people you love. There are many people in the world who
cannot enjoy that pleasure and comfort.

Second, you are a member of a wonderful family who help you
to grow and mature and take care of your needs.

Third, you are blessed with good health and a keen intellect
that is sharp and insightful and quick learning.

Fourth, and very important, you have a delightful sense
of humor and wit that will make your journey through life much

more pleasant and much happier. It will help smooth the rough spots that we all experience.

Fifth, you have a delightful personality that is charming and appealing, and everyone enjoys your company.

The next joy that you can celebrate every day of your life, I did not number it, because it is very special. It is your wonderful brother who is your equal in every way I mentioned above. You both enjoy a special individuality by being equal but different. You are both very lucky to have each other, not only as brothers, but also as friends. And that is your greatest blessing of all.

So, at your 10th birthday milestone, Grandma Myra and I wish you and your brother long life, good health, success and happiness always. We are proud of you, and we love you.

Grandpa Gene

Off to England

August 24, 2001

Dear Scott and Steven,

I am leaving for England tomorrow, Saturday, Aug. 25. I am
going to miss you guys and won't be seeing you for two whole
weeks. Time flies, and before long I'll be back with you again. I
have notes in my luggage to remind me to look for book no. 5,
Harry Potter. If they have it there, I will get it for you. I'll be
taking lots of pictures so you can see just what I'll be seeing. I
hope when you grow up, you are able to travel all over the world.
Our world is an interesting place with different people, different
cultures and exotic venues. When you travel, every day is a new
experience — a chance to grow and learn. Remember, Grandma I
love you both very much, and take care of Daddy and Raellen.

Grandpa Gene

On the Events of September 11th

October 7, 2001

Dear Steven and Scott,

I have waited until now to write to you to allow me time to think more clearly and rationally with less emotion about the events of Sept. 11. All of us look for reasons as to why this happened. Why America? Why now? Who would want to harm America anyway? The answer is as old as civilization itself. There have always been people in this world who want to control others, who want power over other peoples' lives. To us and other freedom-loving people in the world, America means freedom — freedom to worship God in our own way, to vote for our own leaders and government, to move freely around the country and the world. America is a nation of laws that guarantee each of us basic human rights of free speech, the right of assembly, the protection of our person and property, and the privacy of our homes. We are free to pursue our happiness and live our lives any way we wish, as long as we do not infringe upon the rights of others.

The Taliban, who control Afghanistan, dictators like Adolph Hitler, people like Osama Bin Laden see American freedom and way of life as a threat to their power and control over other peoples' lives. They stifle individual initiative, innovation and progress of any kind. They control every facet of their lives, from where people have to work to where they must live. There are no freedoms of any kind as we know it — no freedom of movement, no free press or television, or freedom of information except as they distort and dictate it. Conditions are very harsh, with many shortages of the basic needs of life like food, medicine and good medical care. They invent an enemy, a Satan, to scare the people and subvert religion using God in order to secure firm control over their population. These are evil people, and America and American freedoms frighten them.

In every generation, the enemies of freedom rear their ugly heads, and every time, sooner or later, the people rise up and throw them out. At about the time both of you were born, the peoples of Eastern Europe threw off the yoke of Communism after 75 years of virtual slavery. As long as one man is enslaved in a society against his will, no one anywhere else is truly free. America today stands as a beacon of hope and opportunity to everyone wishing to be free. We as Americans, and with other free people around the world, have an obligation to ourselves and to the oppressed everywhere to defend and promote basic human rights wherever it is denied.

There are many ways we, as young citizens of the United States, can do that. First, be good citizens. When you get older, vote in all the elections, and participate in any way you can in local, state, and federal government and other public and civic groups. Even now, in school, you can participate in many activities where you meet other young people and do things — plan, work and even learn together.

Second, learn to develop your potential as a person. Be all that you can be in our freedom-loving land. Work hard at learning by reading, listening and seeing. You can even look ahead in a general way to where you want to be years down the road. Just think ahead to middle school then high school and college and beyond. Thinking ahead and dreaming of your future is healthy, because it gives you goals to work for and achieve.

Third, and this I know a great deal about, welcome change. Don't be afraid, but expect it. Change is good and refreshing, making life more interesting. As we grow up, we mature; life and circumstances change; seasons and weather change; friends and teachers change; days, months and years change. Nothing remains the same forever. Constant change is part of living. You should welcome it, understand it and adapt to it.

When life seems tough, think of Grandpa Gene, leaving overnight from a comfortable home, living with Great-Grandma Anna and Great-Grandpa William. Then traveling, by train with hundreds of men, to an Army post 1,000 miles away and suddenly thrust into soldiering with thousands of strangers and living in a one room, 45-man barracks. But I adapted and persevered, and in nine months I graduated flight school at 22 years of age as a 2nd Lieutenant Navigator in the United States Air Force. I was qualified to navigate my plane and even groups if we became the lead plane in the skies over America and Asia. I felt that if others could do it, so could I. And I did. I adapted quickly to a new situation, and you can do it too as you grow up.

Fourth, take care of yourself. Maintain your good health and well-being. A healthy person can be an active one with the energy to work hard and be successful. You will then have the ability to enjoy a more complete life and the fruits of your labor.

Fifth, and I find this very important at any age, believe in yourself, in your abilities to do the things you must do to accomplish your goals, and get the job done, whatever that may be. Develop good work habits and be dependable. Your future depends on you alone and no one else. You may get help here and there, but it is still up to you alone. You are both bright and intelligent young men, and you learn quickly. Enjoy your successes, and learn important lessons from your disappointments. There will be some, but keep at it and don't ever give up. In my lifetime, the future has always been brighter than the past, because I made it happen. Like Grandpa, you can and will do the same.

You may ask me now, what has all this to do with terrorism and freedom? Well, nothing and everything. You certainly can't fight terrorism directly. But you can set an example of what one person can accomplish and how far he can develop his gifts and talents by living in a free society. You can enjoy freedom, use its opportunities, flourish with it and thereby protect it for future generations. Freedom is a state of mind, a philosophy of live and let live. As we have witnessed, freedom should never be taken for granted. Preserving it is a continuing effort for all of us — you, Daddy, Raellen, Grandma Myra, me and all Americans.

Grandma Myra and I love you both very much.

Grandpa Gene

On People

January 1, 2002

Dear Steven and Scott,

I can only guide you by what I have learned about life. The idea, of course, is to ease your transition into your teen years, and later into adulthood and into success and personal fulfillment later in life. You know, by now, the emphasis I put upon learning. That effort, and it comes naturally to both of you, never stops. Everything you do, everything you hear and see, wherever you go, teaches you something — about the world, about life, about people, even about yourselves. Your own personal experiences are your best teacher.

   There are two kinds of knowledge. There is so called book knowledge — facts and figures, pure information like we find in an encyclopedia. Then there is people knowledge, how to motivate and influence others, how to get along and cooperate with others in order to accomplish a common or personal goal, how to be a person that others respect and those close to you to love. What you learn and what kind of person you are, are both important for a full and rewarding life.

These two goals, I feel, are easily attainable for both of you. You both learn things and facts quickly and are excellent students. People-learning is a different matter, and it begins with two fine boys like Steven and Scott, whom most people like when they meet you. As you develop your own skills and personality, try to observe other people. You are probably doing that right now. It is a very interesting exercise. Listen to their comments and opinions; see how they act or react. You can tell a lot from their facial expressions, how they gesture and dress, and how and what they say. Often, the less you say, the better.

Only by listening and observing other people do they reveal their thoughts and ideas, how they think, and who they are. You never learn very much by talking, only by listening. There are also other times when you must and should assert yourselves, express your thoughts and make your desires known. It may mean having a true conversation with someone. He or she talks, and then you talk. The trick is to know when to listen and when to talk. You gain valuable experience by being in the company of anyone anywhere and talking with them.

I must give you one word of caution. Never rush to judgment about people or anything. You may have quick opinions, and that may be all the time you get to observe, but always keep your mind open to new ideas. Be flexible, ready to accept new thoughts and facts — you may have good reasons to possibly modify your original opinion about people.

Letters like this should be read now and over again later. They will mean more to you later as you gain experience and wisdom. The next letter that I write to you will be about using your mind. I will discuss how to make decisions, how to solve problems and even how to make learning easier. I will send it to you soon. After that, the ideas about future letters that each of you gave me today will keep me busy for a while. Grandma and I love you both very much.

    Grandpa Gene

The Mind

January 7, 2002

Dear Steven and Scott,

Many of the concepts I talk about in my letters you may already know and use by your natural instincts. The mind is like a computer. You put information in and extract information out. If you tell a computer how, it may even process and interpret it for you. The mind as part of the human anatomy is subject to other human conditions. These include stress, emotions, your general physical condition and your psychological makeup. The intent of this letter is only to give you some practical ideas in using your mind that have served me all my life. They are not unique, but they can help you perform at your best and move your life ahead

Everyone you know, everyone alive, has problems to solve and decisions to make on a daily, hourly or by-the-minute basis. It is a primary activity of living, allowing us to progress with our lives in a coherent manner. Some problems are simple and require very little thought. Just do it. Some are more complex and perhaps more important, even relating to long-term consequences, and require more consideration. What do you do? How do you proceed?

First, recognize this thought. The mind cannot be pushed or coerced; it needs its own time and space. If you force it, it rears up like a stuck animal and will not move. The mind likes to percolate, and, like coffee, the longer it percolates, the stronger and hotter it becomes. Ideas begin to flow, decisions and problems become less formidable and solvable, and you are able to move ahead with your life with renewed hope and confidence.

In solving problems and making decision, you must reduce the conditions that interfere with the thinking process. You must reduce any stress by relaxing, by exercise, reading, listening to music, taking a shower or by talking to someone like your brother, or dad or even a friend. Next, remain calm; your mind cannot work well and honestly in your behalf when you are angry or upset. Also, take care of yourself generally and keep well. A working mind needs a healthy energetic body. Lastly, don't worry or fret about any situation. Many problems actually go away by themselves. Those that don't become easier to deal with the moment you start thinking about them and, more importantly, doing something about them.

You have a problem or must make a decision of some kind. It's time to percolate. Feed the ingredients of your problem into your mind — who, what, when, where, he said, she said, and don't even attempt to find a solution. Put your thoughts on paper if it helps. Let your mind mix it up by itself; let it percolate. You continue to go about your business as usual.

In the quieter moments, like walking, check on the progress your mind is making. Try to look at your problem from different sides. Take your time — do not rush. If I do this, this result may happen; if I do that, something else will occur. Sleep on it. Your mind works even when you sleep. The morning may

offer a solution. Or talk to someone. Verbalizing your problems
with almost anyone helps the thinking process. So does doing
something physical, like exercising, walking or playing ball. Your
mind works all the time.

Soon, you begin to sort things out and make some sense.
Ideas and possible solutions just come forth and, believe it or
not, it works. Some solutions are easy and seem obvious. Some
are questionable or have an element of risk. You then have to
choose the best solution to accomplish what you want. No answer
is perfect. Often your problems involve other people, so consider
your effect on them. But don't be timid. Know what you want,
what's in your best interests, and go for it and keep going for
it. Don't be afraid to make decisions. Any thoughtful decision
is better than no decision. Some may turn out wrong, but many
more will turn out right. You may even decide to do nothing, and
that inaction is also a course of action. That's the way you gain
experience and wisdom. That's the way you grow up and the way
you mature.

Grandma Myra and I love both of you very much.

Grandpa Gene

Self-Confidence

February 11, 2002

Dear Steven and Scott,

Let's talk about self-confidence. If you have it, it can make a big difference in your lives. Confidence gives you the inner strength to attempt all kinds of projects — to be a doer and a learner, to accomplish things, to complete a project despite roadblocks and delay, and to seek out and meet all kinds of people. It can define how you think and how you conduct your lives. What is confidence? How do you know if you have it?

Confidence is a positive state of mind, an optimistic belief in yourself, that you have the ability and the perseverance to do anything you set out to do. Confidence must realistically be based on talents that you know you possess or that you can develop to the point of doing things in a competent manner. Confidence is an accumulation of all the successes and disappointments in your lives, whereby you learn something from all the activities you do anywhere, in school and out. Self-confidence is more than just experience alone. It is continual self-education. Confident persons are better able to change and improve their lives and, thereby, live happier lives.

Confidence is also a discovery of yourself and how you relate personally to the world around you. Just as you learn about the world and the people in it all through your lives, you also learn about yourself, about who you are. You learn what you like or don't like to do, what you can do well and not so well. You learn about what kind of person you are. Are you personable and friendly? Are you dependable and understanding? Do you enjoy doing something very well and like that feeling of accomplishing something worthwhile? Self-confidence is the cement for the building, gas for the car, sunlight for the flowers. It allows you to become the person you want to be.

Grandma Myra and I love you both very much.

Grandpa Gene

To My Great-Grandchildren

April 22, 2002

Dear Great-Grandchildren, grandchildren of Billy, children of Scott and Steven,

This letter was written in April, in the year 2002, by your great-grandfather, Gene Kesselman. It is unlikely that we will ever meet, but Steven thought it would be a good idea for me to write to you, and Scott agreed. God has granted me the privilege of living long enough to have the joy of meeting and knowing Steven and Scott. They are wonderful people by any human measures. You will respect and love them as I do. They are intelligent, personable, understanding and very likeable. They are vital young men, as you will get to know and appreciate even more as you grow up. You will be a credit and a joy to your family and yourselves if you are able to emulate their fine character and personal qualities.

   I was born in 1921 in Newark, New Jersey, and on April 16, I celebrated my 81st birthday [Note: I am now editing this and all the letters for this book in my 96th year in 2016]. I make sure to walk two or more miles most days; I play golf, usually 18 holes; some tennis; I keep expanding my computer knowledge;

continually photograph the people and the world around me; travel overseas every year; and keep active and vital in every way I can. I am five feet, six and a half inches tall, having lost an inch or two as I got older. I have about half my hair left, all white now, and weigh, unclothed, 157 pounds with only a hint of a stomach. I have always tried to take good care of myself and keep thin. My grandchildren and your granddad Billy have lots of pictures of Great-Grandma and me to show you.

Your Great-Grandmother was Myra Lennett before we married on Dec. 28, 1943. We met at Weequahic High School in Newark and used to eat our lunch together. We graduated high school in June 1939. She was born on Jan. 23, 1922, and is now 80 years old. We had two children, David and William, born respectively in 1949 and 1951. I enlisted in the United States Air Force during World War II in 1942, when I was 21 and became a flying officer navigator on a B-24 Bomber on Dec. 24, 1943. I served in the Pacific theatre of operations, in the Philippine islands and in Japan, after they surrendered. After the war, I returned to Rutgers University and graduated at age 27 with a Bachelor of Science degree in marketing in 1948. I later taught marketing, part time, at Rutgers during my 30s to make some extra money. Your granddad, Billy, can fill you in on the rest of my career if you want to know more.

I did not have the money or the time to travel until I was 50 years old. I love to travel, and geography books have always excited me. I went mostly to Europe. Your great-great-grandparents were born there, and our western heritage began and developed in Europe, most particularly in the United Kingdom. My favorite country, though, was Switzerland. The high, snow-covered mountains, the lofty grassy green Alps with a canopy of fluffy clouds and the clear brisk air are citadels of nature that give an imaginative mind a view into eternity. I had one other travel dream, that of going to Nepal and viewing the Himalayan Mountains, the highest in the world, from Pohkara in Nepal. After several attempts, I never managed to make the trip. Steven and Scott have promised to one day fulfill that dream for me.

Let's do some genealogy. I had three brothers; Sam, born 1913; Abe, born 1909; and Sol, born 1907. Sol is the only one still alive today, 2002, at the age of 94 [Note: He died at almost 96 in 2003]. He keeps active, walking, traveling and generally staying busy. His constant advice to me is to keep moving, meaning to stay active and involved. He is the youngest man I know. Steven and Scott have seen him many times and like him a lot. Sol was very impressed with their young yet grown-up maturity. Sol has told his daughter that she would be lucky to have grandchildren as wonderful as Steven and Scott.

My father and mother, William and Anna, your great-great grandparents, were born in Poland in 1883 and were married in America in 1906. My father's mother, your three-greats grandmother, was born in Poland in 1840. My mother's father, Sam Rothbart, died when I was 15 in 1936. He was a big man with a beard and looked very old. He was born in 1851. Let's move on to your great-grandmother on Myra's side. Her mother, Mildred, died in 1969 at the age of 78, and her father, Jacob, died at 84 in 1976. Myra has a sister Shirley, now 83, and not in good health. It is interesting for you to note that you are growing up and building your lives standing on the shoulders of all those wonderful people who have gone before you. You have a rich heritage of accomplishment and good citizenship on which to pattern your lives.

Uncle David, Grandma Myra, Grandpa Gene and Billy heading to a Caribbean vacation in 1965.

Grandpa Gene and his family at his mother's 80th birthday party.

Grandpa Gene and his three brothers with their mother.

Grandpa Gene with Grandma Myra and her family.

Every one of your ancestors has a story to tell, and each one is unique. They have generally lived long and interesting lives, with the inevitable ups and downs that all people experience. What would they say to you now that could guide you in your "pursuit of happiness," as the American Constitution says?

Your granddad Billy, your dads, Steven and Scott, will advise and help you as you grow up. They are wonderful people, and you are very lucky to have them to assist you on your life's journey. However, this is my only opportunity to talk to you. I hope you will be able to understand and take heed of most, or all, of what I have to tell you. Please save this letter and read it again in later years, when you are older, as well as all my other letters to Steven and Scott. They should mean much more to you at that time.

Life is an experience. It is a continuous happening of events and activities, some of which you can control and some that you cannot. What you do, how you react to your surroundings, your mental attitude, and your ability to adjust to and modify events as they unfold will determine the nature and quality of your life. Some of what I have to say to you may not seem relevant to you now. But these common-sense thoughts will help make your growing up easier, your current and future endeavors more successful, and your lives happier and more rewarding, even more interesting.

Most of your knowledge and wisdom as you mature will enter your consciousness through your own trial-and-error life experiences. You learn by doing. This letter is really another "experience" for you from someone who already loves you very much, sight unseen. Much of what I have to say to you is contained in my letters to Steven and Scott. Those letters, written over many years, stand alone, speak for themselves and were also meant for you. You should read them as I originally wrote them. They elaborate on the three paragraphs that follow. Even years later, they will apply equally to you.

The lessons I want to leave for you are simple and direct. Believe in yourself. Be confident in your ability to get the job done, whatever it happens to be at the moment, and to stay with it until it is done well. Learn to be independent and to think independently. Yet seek help if it is necessary, possibly accept help, if it is offered, but ultimately, you must depend only on yourself alone.

Keep learning new things all your life. Learn all you can — from books, from other people, from life's experiences, from both your successes and disappointments. There are lessons to be learned in everything you do. Look for them. That's how you gain experience and wisdom. Listen more than you talk; people like to talk. Allow them that privilege. You can learn much more by listening. Seek the facts and the truth, and think before you open your mouth to speak or decide on any course of action. Remember always that basic knowledge and developed talents are your only true wealth and cannot ever be taken away from you by anyone.

Try hard not to be enslaved by preconceived notions and outmoded truths. Keep an open mind, flexible and open to fresh thoughts and new ideas. Adapt quickly to changes in your life, because changes will happen every day. Be alert for them. Keep busy and active. An unused mind and idle hands soon lose their ability to function well and in time become relatively useless. Continue always to persevere to the best of your ability to help improve your future. Creativity is the only true happiness — doing something, creating something, making something, anything that wouldn't exist unless you did it.

Stay close to your family. They are the best friends you will ever have. Steven, Scott and Grandpa Billy will help light the way for you. They will always love you and believe in you, whatever happens in your life. Great-Grandma Myra and I wish you good luck, good health, happiness and long life, and all our love.

Your Great-Grandpa,
Gene

(Great) Grandpa Gene and his "supper" on duty in the Philippines.

"Officer's Row" on base in the Philippines,
where Gene was stationed.

Disappointment

May 1, 2002

Dear Grandkids,

There are situations that every person, everyone you now know or may ever meet, will experience all through his life. I would like to call them temporary disappointments and momentary failures. These are part of the fabric of our lives and, believe it or not, a valuable and necessary part. I have had more than my share of these unwelcome moments. I call them moments, because if you look at them with the proper attitude as opportunities, you can use them to greatly improve your chances of inevitable success and happiness. They may slow you down for a moment, but you must step over them, move on and continue to work toward your goals.

There are many ways to look at disappointments and failures, and most important of all are the many things you can learn from them. They are always learning experiences at best and time consuming at the least. Don't waste more time wondering what might have been or how unlucky you are. They can teach you right from wrong and better ways to do something. They can show you how to continually modify and improve your approach to any project or problem in order to do a better job. They can teach you about other people, how they think and talk and react to each of you and to your efforts and accomplishments. They even teach you more about yourselves, your level of confidence and your commitment to do better no matter what other people think or say. Weak people use disappointments and failures as reasons to do nothing. Strong people, like the two of you, use them to improve their performance and move on with their daily activities.

What are some common disappointments? Remember, they happen to everyone, not just to you alone. They include the failure to make a team that you try out for, a lower grade on homework or an exam than you expected, a disappointment due to the decisions and even callousness of other people, unflattering remarks directed at you, ordinary happenings like a flat tire on a busy highway or an injury sliding into second base. There are larger ones, like being rejected by the college of your choice, turned down for job you know you are qualified to handle or even by a young lady you want to date.

Nothing that ever happens in life — nothing — means the end of your world. I can tell you from long experience that the best is yet to come. It has always been true for your grandpa because I made it happen, and you can too. When disappointments or failures occur in your lives, you can fret for only 30 seconds. Then start to think and learn. Stand up straight, square your shoulders, take a deep breath and move on.

Let me tell you about one great disappointment that affected my life. After I graduated high school, I took the New Jersey exam for a free state scholarship to Rutgers University. The results were published a month later in the newspapers. I did not pass. I was devastated. I thought my life was over. What would I do? My father didn't have the money to pay my tuition. How would I get to go to college? I fretted for a short while, but I didn't let it beat me.

Uncle Sol came through for me and paid for my first year at Rutgers. Then he got married and had other obligations. With my father's help, I then went to the State Teachers College, now Kean University, just to be able to keep going to school for another year. I didn't want to be a teacher, but it cost very little at that time. If I had gotten the scholarship, I would have gone straight through four years, delayed or canceled my Air Force career and graduated at age 22.

You know the rest. I served my country, as many others did, for almost four years until I was discharged at age 25. I had one main goal, among many others. Go back to college and get an education. I enrolled in Rutgers University, graduating *magna cum laude* at age 27. I went on with my life, and I didn't look back. The past was over, and there was no instant replay.

Understand this. My time in the Air Force was never wasted. I learned many things that I never would have learned anywhere else. I learned a lot about myself and getting along with people, about the value of hard work. At age 24, I was second in command of 1,200 men in the West Airdrome at the air base in Alamogordo, New Mexico. Flying time was cut back, and they had to find jobs to keep us busy. I had to attend staff meetings with generals, because my senior officer, Major Planting, was always indisposed. I was forced to grow up very fast by adapting quickly to every new situation. In the Air Force, that was almost daily. Would my life have been different? Of course it would. Would it have been better? I will never know, and it would not matter anyway. You know about playing cards. I did the best I could with the hand that I was dealt. Always do your best, never complain no matter what the circumstances and never give up.

There is much more to life than disappointments and failures. Look at life and everything that happens to you as full of opportunities. Life is a cornucopia of joy and personally rewarding activity. Even failure, more often than not, happens for the best if you take charge, learn its lessons and do something positive about it. Woe to the men, and there are many of them, who never learn from experience and repeat and repeat their mistakes. George Washington lost many battles during the Revolutionary War, but persevered — despite impossible odds — won the war and helped to establish the United States of America. Abraham Lincoln lost every election he ever entered but persevered until he finally won the election for the presidency of the United States. Franklin Roosevelt contracted polio in 1922, couldn't walk and was confined to a wheelchair for the rest of his life. He persevered and later became governor of New York state and president of the United States in 1932.

It is a wonderful world and a wonderful time to be young. Each age, as you grow up and mature, becomes more rewarding as you apply the lessons of experience and enjoy the pleasures of accomplishments. Cultivate the joy of optimism. It charges the spirit, renews your energy and makes difficult things seem possible. Don't let bad weather or moodiness dampen your enthusiasm, because, like disappointment, it doesn't last very long. Therein lies the lesson of this letter. Every sunrise is the birth of a new day. It is a continuous renewal of spirit and energy with new opportunities to get something done. Each new day makes you wiser than you were the day before. Make good use of it. Grandma Myra and I love you both very much and wish you well.

Grandpa Gene

Computers

June 25, 2002

Dear Billy, Raellen, Steven and Scott,

I guess it was about four years ago that I answered the door in Florida, and there was a UPS man with a box in his hands. It was a laptop computer. I was surprised, happy and nonplussed. I knew nothing about PCs. I looked at it on the table for about 10 days, and then I thought that I better do something about it. I had thought about a computer for myself for a long time, but I didn't know where to start. Anyway, it all seemed too complicated to me — so I did nothing.

Well you folks started it all for me. And your generosity has continued until I now have a powerful desktop with all the latest bells and whistles. I have to struggle to keep up. But then, I always liked a challenge. What it has done is made my spare time useful time and endless hours rewarding hours. It is a wonderful way to keep learning about the world we live in and to keep connected. It is keeping me young. Thank you. I love all of you.

Dad and Grandpa

It's About Time

September 25, 2002

Dear Steven and Scott,

Let's talk about the element of time. I have heard it said that we need time because not everything can happen at once. That certainly makes sense. It takes time to sleep, to eat, to relax, to go to school, to exercise, etc. Doing something, anything, takes time. There are many common sayings about time such as, "You can't do two things at the same time" or "take your time," "time waits for no man," "don't waste time," "there's no time left," and so forth. What makes time so important? Why should it concern you and me, and what can we do about it?

Each and every day, all of us are given 24 hours to use up any way we want. You go to school, Daddy goes to the office and I am retired. There are chores we must do and activities we choose to do. When I get up in the morning, I begin planning my day, and I allot time to accomplish them. It is only a guide, because all during the day I am modifying time slots since life doesn't always follow a plan. I often plan more things than I think I can accomplish so I won't be wasting time. I can always finish them the next day. Yet, so-called free time can also be very valuable.

You don't have to be doing something definitive all the time. Sometimes I take a nap. I may read, take a walk, watch television or just sit quietly somewhere and enjoy nature and think. I am constantly observing the changing world and the people around me and listening to its sounds and voices. It's like a movie that keeps telling a story that never ends, and it doesn't cost a cent.

My life now is different than yours, but we encounter the same problems. My job, at 81, is to stay healthy and keep active. Even as young men, you have the same job. I spend time on my computer, I walk almost every day, I take pictures, I travel when I can, have lunch with my buddies, take care of Grandma, keep up with current events, and I make sure to learn new things every day. I try to keep busy. It is a habit I developed early. It helps to keep me vital and my life always interesting.

At this stage in your life, your use of time is mostly prescribed for you. You go to public school, you study, you play sports, go to Hebrew school, and have some personal and family time. You have little choice now, but that will change as you grow older and as you take greater control of your life and your time. Making good use of your time is only another way of describing an active, meaningful and rewarding lifestyle at any age. The most important thing you can do now is to learn all you can in school and out. It is much easier to learn when you are young. Knowledge and learning will allow you the freedom to be more independent and be more valuable to yourself, your family and your community. Remember, knowledge is your true wealth. The more you know, the richer you are, and I am not talking about money.

Whatever you do, always take the time to do it well. Then you won't have to do it over a second time. Don't delay doing what you are required to do or put it off for later. Later has a way of never being convenient, and other things keep coming up that you have to do. You become pressed for time. You rush and often become overwhelmed. Life and the allocation of time is a balance between what you must do and what you like to do. If they should ever become one and the same, you will both be very lucky young men. That means enjoying your professional life or school as much as you enjoy your recreation time.

I can't really define what time is — to say that "time is time" has no meaning. Then what is time? Well, for one thing, time is an interval between when you start a task and when you finish it. Or time is the interval between sunrise and sunset. Or time is the interval between youth and your senior years. Or time is the difference between now and later. It isn't necessary to define time; it is much more important to know how to use it wisely. Once time is used up, it cannot be retrieved. It doesn't renew itself, or give us a second chance to go back and do a job over, unless we take more time. In a sense, how you make use of your time can define your life — make it rewarding and happy. It is your choice.

Grandma Myra and I love you both very much.

Grandpa Gene

Writing Letters

September 29, 2002

Dear Scott and Steven

It might be interesting for you to know the process I go through
to write these letters to you. It is not that I have all these ideas
in my mind and that all I have to do is write them down. I must
tell you that it isn't easy to distill all the experience of 80-plus
years into a relatively short letter and present it in a practical
and useful manner to your young and maturing minds. After
some time-consuming thinking that may take days or even weeks,
I finally choose a subject that I believe will be both interesting
and at the same time helpful in your growing up and maturing.
My object is to get you to apply many of these practical ideas
to the conduct of your lives and to give you a head start in your
"pursuit of happiness."

   After I have decided on a subject, the next thing I must do is
get something down in writing. It takes about four to eight hours
of intermittent time, again over many days, to get a very rough
draft of ideas that turn out to be disjointed, unconnected and
not in logical form. It takes days, because, as I once wrote to you,
the mind takes its own time, and the good ideas that I can use

do not come all at once. I must dig deep in my mind to dredge up thoughts about subjects that I have not considered for years, if ever. It takes time, but I thoroughly enjoy the exercise.

I have to discard many good, and not so good, ideas that I feel are redundant and do not serve my purpose. It is like a flower that must take time to bloom or like good cheese to get ripe. You would not like that first draft. It is difficult to read. Ideas are repeated, thoughts do not flow logically, and many pertinent points of applying the ideas to your young minds are missing. Yet, that beginning effort is very satisfying to me, because I am filling a blank computer screen and creating an original document that can later be made useful and worthwhile. The more difficult work of shaping and editing that rough draft into a living, coherent letter to my grandchildren must then begin.

I must first consider how your young minds will look at this. You do not have my history of living with these ideas over many days. All of it is foreign to you. I have to develop a logicality of thought to introduce the subject to you, expand it and apply it to your level of maturity, which in many ways is very adult. Then I must sum up its lessons for your lives in a meaningful close. It means that I have to flush out the extra wording and stilted grammar that creeps in when you must quickly verbalize thoughts before they are lost. I take out and add words, rework and switch whole sentences and paragraphs. I cannot fall in love with anything I write. If it doesn't serve my purpose, out it goes. All this takes another four to eight hours. What I strive to accomplish is to have a letter that is logical, easy to read and understand, and that I hope leaves a lasting impression while remaining relatively short.

The purpose of this letter is to impress on your young minds that good results can only come from hard work and perseverance. Writing these letters is not easy, but I thoroughly enjoy the challenge. It allows me to create something that I hope will have lasting value to you, my grandchildren and your children.

Whatever project you may ever have in school or out, now or in the years to come, take the time to think it through first and decide what you will require and what you must do to accomplish your goal. Then do the best you can and give it all you've got. Stick with it until you, and only you, are completely satisfied with the results. Never rush it through or settle for second best.

Grandma Myra and I love you both very much.

Grandpa Gene

My Childhood in America

October 15, 2002

Dear Steven and Scott,

This letter travels back 80-plus years in time, to an America with 55 percent fewer people. It was just a few years after World War 1, on April 16, 1921, that my life began in a bedroom, attended by a midwife, in a two-family house on 17th St. in Newark, New Jersey. I was born into a different country than the one we have today. It was a far simpler society with fewer gadgets and without many things we now consider commonplace. If either of you were suddenly dropped into the middle of 1920s America, you might think you were in a third-world country.

Traffic jams were relatively unknown, since there were less than 10 percent of the cars we have on the roads today. The early cars looked like horse-and-buggy wagons without the horses. A new car could cost as much as $400. Everyone took buses to get around town and travel to downtown where all the big, and only, department stores and first-run movies were located. Anything you needed from food to clothing to everything else was sold at small stores in your neighborhood near your home. The city was peppered with these compact and complete entities.

The neighborhoods were so compact that children could

walk to their school. There was no such thing as the suburbs. Outside the city, you were out in the country. Randolph was the wilderness. My public school was right across the street from our two-family house at 2 Farley Ave., on the corner of Avon Ave., that my dad owned in Newark. We moved there in 1923, when I was two, and from which I left for the Air Force and World War II in March 1943. We lived in a large three-bedroom apartment on the second floor. I could hear the school bell ring for class from my bedroom. I also walked to my junior high that was over a mile away — two round trips a day to include lunch. School buses were unknown.

There were no shopping or strip malls anywhere, nor supermarkets or chain stores like Wal-Mart or Home Depot. Most stores were small, family run, with personal service to each customer. You waited your turn. Every neighborhood had a full complement of necessary stores, like food, hardware, bakery, five-and-dime, household goods, etc. You couldn't wander around the store and pick what you wanted. You waited at a counter, and the salesman brought you most of what you asked for. You had to carry everything home. It was very rare to take a car to go shopping, if you even owned one, because the stores were so close.

The product choices were very limited. My mother had to shop for food almost every day. Frozen foods only began to arrive in the mid 1930s, so there was no way to store foods for long periods of time. We cooled our perishables in an icebox. Every day or two, the iceman, Mr. Katz, would arrive in front of our house with his horse and wagon loaded with chunks of ice. There were a great many horse and wagons used in those days. The streets were the lucky recipients of plenty of horse manure, and we stepped in it all too often. My mother would place a sign in the window indicating the size of ice she wanted, 10, 15 or 25 cents worth. He would then carry it up to our second-floor apartment, carrying it on his back with ice tongs. Milk and other very perishable foods would lie right up against the ice.

Every night we would empty the melted ice water pan, or it would overflow onto the kitchen floor and often did. Our first fridge arrived in 1932 with the round motor exposed on top. I'll never forget it. Great-Grandma Anna was in heaven. She sat and looked at it for hours and listened to the steady hum of the motor. It made her life much easier cooking for five men, your Great-Grandpa Willie and their four sons. Poor Mr. Katz — technology put him out of the ice business.

There were few packaged foods, certainly not like today. Butter came in 50-pound tubs, and the grocer would gouge out a chunk, weigh it and wrap it in white paper. Many foods came in bulk, like butter. There were barrels around the store filled with nuts, dried fruit, cookies, crackers, cereal, etc. Packaged foods were rare. Bottled milk was kept outside the store in a solid wooden box painted blue, filled with ice and protected by a padlock.

One new concept supermarket finally opened in Newark in 1932. It was called The Big Bear. The whole of North Jersey went crazy. Imagine walking around among the shelves alone with your own cart and picking out what you wanted. It was the sensation of the times. Yet many people didn't like it. It was too impersonal and unfriendly. Of course it was crowded; and you needed a car to drive there and many didn't own one. You had to drive miles through the city. Then, after shopping, carry your bundles to the car. Where were you going to store all the stuff you bought? It took many years to develop the full concept of supermarkets as we know it today, and just as long for home sizes, storage areas and home refrigeration to catch up. Most of us lived in multiple apartment dwellings with very little storage area. Only the very rich lived in one-family homes. As you can see, many new ideas take time to germinate and more time to understand their significance and to afford to integrate them into our lives.

Here is one interesting market that I remember vividly. My mother would go to a chicken market to buy chickens once a week. She made the same meal, chicken soup and boiled chicken, every Friday night for Great-Grandpa Willie, including carrots and lima beans. The market consisted of a large open area — straw on the floor and one side enclosed with chicken wire to form a pen. Inside were live chickens, clucking, flying around and making a mess. I wouldn't go in; live chickens scared me. Great-Grandma Anna had to pick out a chicken after they showed her a few, and they killed it right there in front of us. They pulled out the feathers and cut off the toe nails, bagged it, and she took it home while it was still warm. Great-grandma, at home, had to hold the naked chicken over an open gas flame on the kitchen stove, to burn off the residual feathers, before she could even begin preparing it for cooking. As you can see, life in those days was not nearly as convenient and easy as it is today.

There were no intercity limited-access highways like the Turnpike or the Garden State Parkway, just roads built like city streets that went through the center of every city on the route. Intercity traffic competed with local traffic on the same roads. They were often very crowded on weekends and holidays and slow because of traffic lights and no available alternate routes. A trip to the Jersey Shore took a couple of hours. Roadside restaurants, like McDonalds or Burger King, were unknown. You took your own food and drink on a trip.

One of our treats at that time was the weekend auto ride with no destination in mind, just a ride in the country. At that time, Caldwell was the mid-west, and Randolph was the far west and very rural. People with respiratory and other ailments were sent to Caldwell for the clean, fresh country air to recuperate. How clean and fresh is it today?

After World War II ended in 1945, developments started to accelerate. The interstate road system like Route 80 began to be built in the 1950s. The U.S. population began to soar due to returning soldiers wishing to start new lives interrupted by the war and more immigration from foreign countries. Then the baby boomers, like Daddy, started coming along. As you know I went back to college and graduated at age 27. My generation had a rough time. The war made us grow up fast, and we started our careers four and five years later than normal. Up to 15 million men came back to a different America in a relatively short time, with many shortages like cars, housing and appliances caused by the need for wartime production. It took many years for the supply to catch up with demand.

It is a much faster world today, and the impact of new technology makes things happen quicker. Today, the world is more mobile with more automobiles, roads and jet planes to move us around faster. Communications are instantaneous; TV gives us real-time pictures from everywhere in the world. Cell and mobile phones keep us in touch with anyone anywhere. Computers store and process information in quantities we could only dream about. All of this science fiction stuff was totally unknown back then.

Let me tell you a short tale. When I was your age I had a friend, Ted Goldstein, who always had a dollar or two with him. That was big money for a kid to have. Remember an ice cream cone cost only five cents. I never had more than a few cents or maybe as much as nickel, if I was lucky. I never received a regular allowance. A quarter would have made me a rich kid. Uncle Sol would sometimes give me a quarter to shine his shoes or run an errand for him. Well, Ted one day received a tabletop radio. Even then, the radio was very new. We kept them only in the living room as cabinet furniture, and the family used to sit there quietly for hours just to listen. When I was younger radios operated only on batteries, and when they ran down the radios stopped working. A tabletop plug-in radio, the Emerson, that came along later was a tremendous sensation. Imagine, you could carry it around and place it in any room you wanted. Ted put his new radio next to his bed. I ran home excited as the devil and told my mother about it. What a big treat it was just to lie on Ted's bed and be able to listen to a radio that wasn't in the living room.

That was then and this is now. America and the world have come a long way in the last 60 or 70 years. Can you even begin to imagine how the rest of the world looked 70 years ago? America has 275 million people now, about double at the time I was born. I grew up at a simpler time and served in a war far from home. I look at things from a different perspective based on a different background and time frame.

I cannot change the past — no one can. I have learned that the many decisions we make in life have certain results, some that may take years for us to discern. I have been very lucky to have to have been granted those additional years and to have witnessed the results of my actions, good and otherwise. I have always tried to learn some lesson, some truth, even about myself, from everything I have ever done or experienced. This is the most important lesson I can ever leave to you. Every experience in life, whatever it may be, success or disappointment, happy or unhappy, has some learning value. Make sure you look for it.

As I approach my 82nd birthday, I still look and plan ahead as I have always done. My greatest joy is to have two wonderful grandsons as wise and intelligent as you and to be able to impart something of who I am and what I have learned in a long and active life. I am very proud of your young wisdom, and I know, even now, how each of you will use it to live full and productive lives.

Grandma Myra and I love you both very much.

Grandpa Gene

Scott's Bar Mitzvah

November 2, 2002

Dear Scott,

It is with a great deal of pride and joy that we celebrate your bar mitzvah on November 16, 2002. We say pride because of the wonderful person that you are, and joy because you have achieved an important milestone in your life. You can now join a minion — become one of 10 men necessary to conduct a Jewish religious service. In the Jewish sense, you have become a man. You are a member of the world's oldest living religion and an heir to thousands of years of learning and survival.

Survival then becomes a key word, and just for us to survive is considered an achievement in itself. You have survived to your 13th birthday, your dad to his 51st, and your Grandpa to his 81st. Yet for us Jews, the effort to survive over the years against all odds has made us the people we are. Throughout the millennia, our predecessors have had to overcome impossible challenges to their livelihood, their thoughts and their very existence. During that time, hundreds and maybe thousands of civilizations and cultures on every continent have flourished for a while and then disappeared. What is the secret that makes it possible for one group of people not only to maintain their identity but to prevail for that long a period of time?

In truth, it is really no secret at all. It is people, Scott, people like you, since the values and achievements of the human family can only begin with the individual. You should be aware that you strive not only for yourself, but for all the generations that will follow you. You are my first grandchild and your dad's first son to become a bar mitzvah and inherit our legacy. It is our good fortune to be allowed to see the future through your eyes and your mind. All of us who love you take great pleasure in watching your progress as you mature in your early years. You are enabled to build your life standing upon our shoulders and extending your own horizons well beyond ours.

The proud heritage you represent is a gift from our generations to yours. It is not enough just to treasure it; you must contribute and add to it. Developing your full potential as a human being is the only way to reach that goal. You have the ability to learn, to think and to accomplish whatever you set out to do. I like to think there is a measure of greatness in each us. I don't mean by becoming president or by climbing the highest mountain, but by doing the things that make up our daily lives in a competent and effective manner.

Spend your time wisely, be curious, persist in worthwhile tasks, continue to be kind and considerate, honor truth, be a good friend, and love all those who love you and wish you well. God bless you and your family. Mazel tov and love from Grandma and me.

Grandpa Gene

P.S. – I want Steven to know and understand that whatever I have said about Scott in the letter above applies equally to him.

Grandma and I love you both very much.

GG

Growing Up

January 15, 2003

To Steven and Scott,

Steven's suggestion that I tell you about my early years requires me to temporarily abandon my normal orientation toward the future and reverse course back to the past. I enjoy taking pictures only to remember the look of the past, but not the thinking, the uncertainties and the emotions of long ago. We are nostalgic for old times, because it reminds us of family and friends who may no longer be available to us. The only immutable fact is that we were younger then, and that makes it seem better then maybe it actually was. In truth, those earlier years were possibly no happier or more satisfying than the present and perhaps less so in many ways. My lifelong motivation has always been based on the idea that the best is yet to come, and then to persist in my efforts to make it come true. So I will begin this personal journey backward and hope that I can present it to you as honestly as I can remember it 70 or more years later.

I was a shy, young boy, pleasant, placid and quiet. I often heard my mother tell others that I was the easiest of her four sons to raise. With three older brothers, my voice could scarcely be heard. At the time I was going into kindergarten, Sam, who was eight years older, was entering high school; Abe, who was no student, was working; and Sol was already in college. My father came to this country from Poland at 21 and could not read or write. With his foreign background, there was very little we could discuss about my future or life in America. Each of my brothers was too busy developing their own future. It often seemed to me that I was an only and lonely child.

As a youth I read a great deal. In a sense, reading was my escape, and it helped to open the world to me. I was at the library several times a week, returning books that I read and getting new ones. Everyone in those days had time to spare with no television, computers and with far less mobility than today. Where would you go? There were no malls, shopping centers, mega movies or superstores. In my youth, there were no little leagues or after school events. Most people came home after work or school and stayed home. When you called someone on the phone, they always answered. There was no such thing as an answering machine.

It was a less complicated time, with much more time for family and friends. You visited in their homes or yours if you wanted to get together. I had plenty of time to read and learn and to think. Yes, I played ball and street games and hung out in the neighborhood with the guys, but I was hungry for knowledge. My mind, I think, developed faster than my body. I became a good student and a fast learner. I placed seventh academically in my high school graduating class of 432 students. Our student quotations committee picked the following phrase that was printed under my picture in the high school yearbook: "The mind to conceive, the heart to understand and the hand to execute."

Let's move ahead a few years, to near the end of my military service. You already know something about my years in the Air Force. It is now May 1946. I am in Tokyo, Japan, after being transferred from Manila in the Philippine Islands in February. I am the officer in charge of land transportation (the motor pool) at the Tachikawa Army air base, 25 miles north of Tokyo. I persuade the new chief personnel officer to place me on orders to return to the United States. I had befriended him by assigning him the use of a personal jeep when he arrived from Manila the previous month. He somehow finds the authorization in some obscure Air Force regulation, and by the middle of the month I am on board a troopship with hundreds of other returning military men at the port of Yokohama. I wanted to be home in time to register at college for the fall term, or I would lose an entire academic year. It sails at noon for Seattle, Washington, and I am finally on my way home. I had served overseas five months in the Philippines and three months in Japan.

Serving in the military during a war had changed me and my view of life. I was no longer placid and quiet. I had seen too much, met too many people and was sent to too many strange places. In many ways, it was an exciting time, living through fast-moving events and waiting each day for new military orders that would change your current situation. You lost and made friends with every change. You could never permit yourself to get too comfortable, because your destiny was controlled by others. Your mind had to be flexible and fully packed at all times, ready to move on at a moment's notice to something new or somewhere else. Rumors were our morning newspaper, and they had a large circulation. Once on the ship, I had to shed my military cocoon and begin taking back my life. It was no easy task.

I was 25 years old with a minimum of two more years

of college to finish. How could I decide what courses to take if I could not decide what I wanted to do? I had no specialized knowledge that I could build upon to allow me to earn a reasonable living. I was trained as an aerial navigator. Navigators were not needed in post-war America with the new technologies that had been developed. My discharge certificate listed dozens of specific jobs and duties I had performed in the Air Force, and I could not apply any one of them to the commercial world. As I pondered these and other questions sailing across the Pacific, new ideas began to percolate in my mind.

During my Air Force years, I was able to observe the actions and reactions of literally thousands of men and women under all kinds of conditions, some extremely stressful. They were men with whom I had worked, lived and trained. They were officers serving above me in command positions that I reported to and men in groups that I had commanded and reported to me. It also included a rescued Philippine population who had experienced tremendous horror and devastation at the hands of the Japanese and the heavily bombed Japanese islands, just conquered and occupied, and now ruled by Americans like me. I had my own jeep in both places. I would travel around the surrounding countryside when I was off duty, either alone or in the company of others, and observe firsthand the profound effects of war on people and property. I also joined sightseeing tours for military personnel that included many famous World War II battlegrounds. It was a picture window on a war-torn part of the world.

The one activity that pervaded my military experience was my continuous interaction with new people. They were Americans from every corner of our country and from all walks of life and military men from our allies, Filipinos and Japanese.

Grandpa Gene at age 15.

Grandpa Gene on duty in the Philipinnes, 1945.

Gene (2nd from right) with fellow officers in
Salt Lake City, Utah, enroute overseas.

It seemed to me that the war had matured me in ways I could never have imagined when I entered service. I wanted to be able to utilize that vast learning experience and continue that interaction with people in my chosen field of endeavor. This is how and why I chose advertising, sales and marketing to make my fortune. These were people-oriented activities, in which I could attempt to influence their thinking and their motivations. By the time I arrived in Seattle, I had decided on my college major and had planned my immediate future. I was discharged at Fort Dix, New Jersey, in June of 1946, and entered Rutgers School of Business in September. I graduated in June of 1948 at the age of 27 with a Bachelor of Science degree in business administration with a major in marketing. A few years later, I was teaching these same subjects at Rutgers part time, in addition to my other jobs.

In the many years since, I have always felt that I would have been happy and successful in almost any field I chose. I would have been a good doctor, lawyer, scientist, concert pianist or even an explorer traveling to faraway places. Yet we live in a practical world, and you have to make practical decisions based on the truth as you determine it at the time. The past is gone forever. You can only learn something from it and hopefully gain some wisdom. You cannot go back and change anything. That is why my focus has always been to the future. Even now I think about my next trip, my next car and my growing grandchildren with their lifetime ahead of them.

Grandma Myra and I love you both very much, and we wish you a future of good health and good choices.

Grandpa Gene

Truth

May 25, 2003

Dear Steven and Scott,

The court clerk says to the witness, "Do you swear to tell the truth, the whole truth and nothing but the truth, so help you God?" The witness says, "yes," and the clerk then tells the witness to be seated. This scenario is repeated thousands of times a day in courts all over America and perhaps in different forms all over the world.

There are many things we know to be true. We know that water freezes at 32 degrees and boils at 212 at sea level, that the sun rises and sets each day at precise times. All of us agree on these and millions of other proven facts. There are untold millions of people all over the world who spend their lives in research looking for the truth in medicine, science, the environment, human behavior and any other factual information that can add value to our lives. But the truth I am emphasizing here is the truth, variations of the truth or the total lack of it that influences our relationships with the people we meet or with whom we share our daily lives. Let us call it human behavior truth.

Think of this. Two people witness a car accident. Person A
says that car X ran into car Y, and person B says car Y ran into
car X. Which is telling the truth? Each one is convinced he is.
Which one do you believe? As you begin to see, determining the
truth can get very complex and difficult to determine. Where
were A and B located in relation to the accident? Possibly they
were not together and their angles of viewing the accident
were different. Does either one have poor eyesight or any health
problems that could affect their observations? Had either one
ever been involved in an accident previously that might affect
their reactions to this accident? What is their age and the age
of those in the cars? People near the same ages have an affinity
for each other. That, and many other related factors, can affect
their interpretation of what they believe they witnessed. I think
you get the idea.

Twelve people on a jury hear the same evidence and have
difficulty agreeing on a verdict. Any number of people can
witness the same scene or event, and each one sees it differently.
Put six, eight, 10 people in a room, whisper a brief story or a
statement into one's ear and let each pass it on to their neighbor
quietly ear to ear. What you will hear at the end from comes out
very differently and often unrecognizable from the original. Each
individual has put his own personal spin on it. That should tell
you a great deal about the validity of gossip and the truth.

Every court in the world is constituted to search for the
truth. When the trial is over the judge must render a decision
based on what he perceives the truth to be. Juries spend endless
hours in the jury room after a case is argued in the courtroom
discussing their individual perceptions of the truth as presented
by both sides. One jurist thinks the defendant is guilty, and
another thinks he is not guilty. I have been in a jury room. You

would be amazed at the different reactions and the disparate interpretations of the same information. It would seem that some jurists who had listened to the same testimony were never really in the courtroom at all.

What is truth? That simple question may be difficult for anyone to answer with any certainty. You would think that in any situation there is only one real truth, the facts, immutable and unquestionable. As you see the truth can be very elusive, and it can often be impossible to determine. Other people may interpret the same facts or observe the same events differently than you. Therefore, your understanding of the truth may not be the same as someone else's. As a result, the truth can wear many different coats and come in varied shades, colors and sizes. It can hide behind or be distorted by prejudice, greed, pride, ambition and many other human qualities, both good and bad. Truth, like beauty, is often in the mind of the beholder.

Your understanding of what the truth is will guide your efforts the rest of your life. Almost every decision you will make will be based on facts that you believe are true. When someone tells you something, is he telling the truth? He may honestly believe he is. Can you base important or even minor decisions in life on the things that people tell you? Think of this: Will your actions based on what they tell you affect them in any way? A significant part of your life will be spent in determining the truth to your satisfaction and most particularly when it is important to your welfare. There are many ways that you can attempt to find the truth for yourself.

You can see it with your own eyes, touch it with your own hands or talk to many others involved or those who should know. Compare their stories and then apply what you have learned and your own good sense to help you make a decision or solve your problem. Don't depend totally on any one version of anything, whether it's people, books, the internet or whatever. In gathering information, there is safety in numbers, and always try to use many sources.

Let me close this letter with the following observations. Life never has to be overly complicated if you know some of the rules of good-sense behavior and understand the human mind and how it works. I have found that most circumstances in life are never as good as they seem or never as bad as they seem. There is usually no true black or white, only shades of gray. When any circumstance or the deal look too good, seek some of the downside. Believe me, it's there. Conversely when things look discouraging, there is probably some upside, if only for the experience. Take the extra time to look at both sides. You will never be too surprised or unprepared if you search for the truer picture, and you will be able to cope with the future more successfully as it unfolds. These practices will give both of you a far more satisfying life and a happier one too.

Good luck in all your endeavors and good health. Grandma Myra and I love you both very much.

Grandpa Gene

Young Grandpa

July 22, 2003

Dear Steven and Scott,

It is difficult for me to believe that I was once a teenager and before that a preteen and before that a baby. It must be true, because I have the pictures to prove it. What kind of boy was I, and what did I think about? When you get older, you think you were always the way you are now. I have traveled a long road, and over the course of my busy life, I have tried to learn something of value from every twist and turn. I have been blessed with a high energy level and a curious and alert mind. Even as a youngster I was always sensitive to what was going on around me physically and emotionally. Growing up I have vivid memories of hundreds of encounters with my parents, brothers, relatives, friends and all those they came in contact with in my presence. In the company of so many adults I could say very little, but I could listen and observe.

I have been told that I was very contented as a baby, and that I seldom cried. I could play by myself for hours and bother no one. The earliest memory I have is standing in my crib in my parents' bedroom, holding the railing and dancing on my toes.

My mother told me that she once gave me her wedding band to play with, and after a while I threw it out a nearby open window. We lived on the second floor of a two-family house and it was never found. She wore an inexpensive substitute ring for the rest of her life. Another memory is of being carried by my father into Dr. Barkhorn's office at the age of two or maybe four to have my infected ear treated. It was a cloudy, cool day. I had a fever, and I was wrapped in a blanket. My father held me tightly as the doctor lanced my eardrum to relieve the pressure of the infection. It was a sharp, fast pain, and then it felt better. I had that same problem three times by the time I was 18.

I remember Dr. Reich, when doctors made house calls, charging into my bedroom to treat my case of measles, swinging his medical bag. He had a halo of thinning white hair, and his big tall body filled the door opening. I thought he was God. When he sat on my bed, it sagged so much I almost fell out. I have a vivid memory of my mother lighting a special medicinal candle when I had the whooping cough. It was supposed to help me breathe. My coughing was so violent at times that I couldn't catch my breath, and I could literally suffocate. She slept next to me for a week. When I had a coughing spell, she would quickly pull me up and raise my arms over my head to keep me from choking. As you can see, there were some interesting childhood diseases around when I was young.

We lived in a two-family house at the corner of Farley and Avon Avenues. Avon Avenue was a busy street with lots of noisy traffic. I could see Avon Avenue School and play yard from my bedroom, and I could hear the school bell ring the beginning and change of classes. Many times, I made class just in time. We moved there when I was 2 years old, and I left when I went into the Air Force in 1943 at the age of 21. I have never lived there again. During the war, my folks shut off the front part of our large apartment with three bedrooms and two dens to conserve scarce fuel for the war effort.

Most homes in Newark were multiple dwelling units, and they were close together, with just narrow alleys between them, and had small backyards. The population density was high, with lots of families and lots of kids. The average city block had from 40 to 60 families and often more. In the suburbs where people began to move in the years after the war, the average block would have only eight to 15 families living in one-family homes more widely separated from each other. It was a congested and different kind of life. Your world was confined to a few blocks. Almost everything you needed was within walking distance. You could walk to school, any friend's house, the movies, the library and shop for almost anything.

There were many factories in our congested inner-city neighborhood. As a child, I used to think their whistles, which signaled the change of work shifts, actually blew from the clouds. It was strange to me that they didn't blow on weekends and that they sounded on days when there were no clouds.

When I began kindergarten, I would throw up several times a week. It was usually under the metal mesh stairs leading from the schoolyard up to my classroom. Mrs. Fader, a neighbor, remembers my mother's distress as to how to help me. She said it was Mrs. Stansbury's fault, as my teacher she was harsh and mean. I remember at one time attempting to put on my winter coat. When my mother tried to help me, she pushed her away and told her to let me struggle by myself.

I was the youngest of four brothers by eight years, and as a youth I was alone a great deal. I had plenty of time to think, read and dream. I read because it transported me anywhere I wanted to be. It filled up my mind with other people, places and happenings, both fictional and real. All we had then was the radio. There were no TVs, computers, DVDs, cell or cordless phones, video players, electronic or digital anything. I couldn't wait to listen to Admiral Byrd's weekly broadcast from his expedition at Little America in frozen Antarctica at the bottom of the world. It came in scratchy and full of static. But it was a voice from a faraway place, and I was fascinated. The library was my window on the world, and I was there many times a week. My curiosity was insatiable.

When the evening paper came, the comics were the second thing I read. I couldn't wait to check the marine list of passenger liners sailing in and out of busy New York Harbor. It included their ports of call, places from all over the globe. I knew the names and sizes of most passenger vessels sailing our part of the world. At that time, it took one week to sail to Europe and another week back. Air travel was in its infancy and not yet walking. Travel by public conveyance anywhere, even in America, was slow, time consuming and expensive, and only wealthy people could afford it. Is it any wonder that your grandpa loves to travel and see new places? Today, thanks to your dad, I have a computer, and I can travel the world over in seconds.

In winter after a big snow, we sledded down steep Madison Avenue, a three-block run. We had to be very careful about cars crossing from the side streets. There were many close calls, and I had my share. At the end of many a day of playing outside, my father's shrill whistle using four fingers, that could be heard a full block away, would summon me home. I remember the day I graduated from high school. When I returned home, my brother Sam had a big poker game on the front porch. He looked up at me and asked where I had been. I told him that I had just come from my high school graduation. He looked surprised, reached into his playing money, handed me a five-dollar bill and told me to buy myself something. He then returned to his game. I don't recall if he said anything appropriate or not. No one else said a word.

I played all the games of that day, touch football, softball, stickball and others. I was competitive, and I always played hard. I never cared much for youthful mischief. Remember, this was the inner city, and there were always plenty of kids around. When the other guys wanted to do something raunchy for excitement, I usually hung back and never really participated in their escapades. At Halloween, I dressed up and trick-or-treated with the guys. I played marbles in the schoolyard and climbed behind the garages to play war. I tore my share of pants, got some bad cuts, but I never broke any bones. At 14, I began piano lessons for a few years. That gave me a lifelong love of that instrument and music in general.

As I think back now, I guess I was kind of an intellectual kid. Even then I would rather talk with someone and exchange ideas than do almost anything else. I enjoyed plenty of bull sessions as I grew up with other kids, hanging out at the corner candy store or on someone's front porch. I learned about them, their dreams and thoughts. I always listened more than I talked. In listening you learn, and in talking you formalize and commit your thoughts. Always think carefully before you express your thoughts and ideas, because you expose your mental underwear to your listeners.

I cultivated an interest in other people and their thinking, which fascinates me to this day. It helped me develop my own personal philosophy and my place in this world. You cannot help but draw comparisons between you and them, and I knew then that I could never be just one of the guys. I always felt that I thought differently and deeper than most people. That has always limited me to a few close friends.

All my life I have always kept busy. I am a restless man, and I am easily bored. I need challenges like writing these letters, learning new things on the computer, observing and photographing the world around me, and the excitement of traveling to new places. The grass could never grow high under my feet.

At the age of 41, two weeks after Christmas and two weeks before Uncle David's bar mitzvah, I lost my job. While my boss was telling me the bad news, I quickly thought of a plan to turn possible disaster into an opportunity. I talked him into letting me sell their line and use their car temporarily until I could buy my own car. At that moment I went into business as an independent manufacturer's agent. I was now my own boss, and it turned my life around. I would never work for anyone else again. After 17 years of success, that business finally fizzled when I lost a major line and 65 percent of my income. I wasn't ready to give up and retire to a rocking chair. At the age of 58 when most men are dreaming about retirement, your dad and I together started Oak Tree in my West Orange home. A whole new opportunity opened up for both of us. We were immediately successful, because we worked hard and smart. We quickly learned the ins and outs of a brand new business and took advantage of every opportunity to prosper and grow the business.

Any man's life is worthy of a book. Each of us has much to share. Often I have taken the time to assess my life: Where am I now, how did I get here and where am I going? It can be an interesting exercise, and I have realized many things that have made my long road, in a lot of ways, somewhat easier and even happier. I look upon each of you as my young self, and I envy your trip. Your future is full of promise, excitement, activity and reward. I know you can do it, because you have the stuff.

Grandma Myra and I love you both very much.

Grandpa Gene

Photography

August 4, 2003

Dear Scott, Steven, Raellen and Billy,

Photography can be described as the artistic expression of the
average person, usually those with little or no artistic talent.
Most of us cannot paint, draw or sketch the world as we see it in
any realistic way. If we wish to make a visual record of what we
see, we must acquire a camera and take a picture. The very act
of taking a picture makes us artists nevertheless, and our camera
then becomes our paintbrush and our sketch pad.

Why do any of us take pictures? Is it to express our
individuality in some personal way, or are we like the artist
whose only desire is to make a statement about how he views the
world? For most of us, our only purpose may be to preserve just
what unfolds before us and nothing more. The artist, meanwhile,
has the option of distortion, exaggeration, symbolism, and
infinite variations of mood and color. He can change the entire
reality of what he observes and allow us to see only his altered
conception. That is his art and his purpose. You, as an amateur
photographer, have fewer options. The scene you see is more
often the only reality you want to record, generally for yourself,

friends or your family. That is your art.

Pictures are reliable witnesses to our past. They remind us of who we were and of our long journey to who we are today. One old picture seen years later can resurrect a thousand thoughts of nostalgia and joy and perhaps regret. I have found that I can revive long-forgotten memories of trips, events and people more vividly only in the context of the pictures I have taken. That is my singular reason for making a visual record of my life, the people I meet and the changing world around me. As you get older, you will often wonder where all the years have gone. They seem to fly by all too quickly. Pictures allow me to enjoy the continuity of my life and prove to myself that I wasn't just born and suddenly arrived at today overnight.

I have often felt that people who enjoy taking pictures on a regular basis share many similar endearing qualities. They are sentimental and they have more heart, else why bother at all about the past? They are more caring and take greater pleasure in being with and even helping other people, else why photograph them? Most of all they are more aware of the world's natural beauty, because their minds and their eyes seem to constantly seek pictorial opportunities. We inveterate photographers look at our surroundings through prisms of realism and humanism. We are historians as well as artists.

I began taking pictures at around 20 years of age. My first camera was a boxlike, bulky, no frills Argus C-3, and I was thrilled to have it. All of my Air Force black and white 35-millimeter pictures were taken with it. When Kodachrome slide film arrived in the mid '40s, I bought it immediately. It was a sensation at the time, and I have taken the thousands of slides that all of you are enjoying today. Over 20 years ago I switched to Kodak Color print film, and I have thousands of pictures filed as to time and place. Over the years, I have progressively owned about 20 cameras, each one representing the latest technology. Today, of course, digital cameras and computers are changing the face of photography dramatically, and allowing us to greatly expand our freedom of expression and control. I can't wait to see what innovations are coming along next.

More than 10 years ago, I met a lady who had been married to the son of a former resident of my father's European hometown. It was at a dinner for the descendants of Gombin, Poland, and their families. She walked up to me and remarked that we had gone to Avon Avenue School together. I didn't recognize her at all until she mentioned her name. I remembered her instantly and also recalled that as children in kindergarten we would walk in pairs holding hands. I once walked with her, and remembered that her hands were as rough as sandpaper. She said she had the picture of our public school graduating class and would be happy to send it to me a copy.

It came three weeks later and slightly out of focus, with the names of all the graduates on a separate sheet. I was overjoyed at seeing most of the faces I haven't seen in almost 60 years. I could only match half the names with faces. There I was at 14 in the top row surrounded by Ziggie, Puggy, Harry, Danny, Violet, Margaret and all the other guys and gals with whom I spent so many of my earliest years. Every couple of months I take the picture out again and look at it. I wonder where they are today and how their lives have turned out. Many of them have passed on. After a while I put the picture away, always realizing that the only reality is now. I can remember the past, but I cannot live in it.

We may look at most of the pictures we take only once or twice and never again, but we know they exist and are available.

Please take the time to photograph your fellow classmates, friends, relatives, teachers and the people you meet and like on your long journey through life. They will never remain the same. Photograph your surroundings, your homes, school and places you visit. They will change, or even cease to exist, and you will move on. With pictures you can never lose your past to a fading memory, and you will always be older than any picture you ever took.

Grandma Myra and I love all of you very much.

Grandpa Gene

Mountains

August 29, 2003

Dear Scott and Steven, Raellen and Billy,

My love of mountains began at a very early age. I must have been one to two years old when my brother Sol brought a geography book home from Cleveland Junior High School in Newark. It remained around the house for a long time before I knew enough to take a look at it. There was a chapter in it on Switzerland with black and white pictures of the Alps. It fascinated me so much that every time I opened the book afterwards, I would be drawn to that section. Since I was not yet able to read, I would just enjoy gazing at the pictures. That book and my early love of mountains have remained a part of me all my life. It has grown stronger as I grew up and I was finally able to travel and see my dream mountains for myself.

What is there about mountains that make them such a subject of awe and joy not just for me but also for countless others? In deciding to write this letter to you, I began to think definitively for the very first time of some of the possible reasons for my obsession.

Grandpa Gene in Murren, Switzerland, overlooking the Eiger, 2005.

Mountains rise above the surrounding lowlands either as a loner or huddled in groups known as ranges. As the night moves aside for the day, they wake up as you and I do and dress for the new day's weather, openly and silently. It could be the sun's warming rays, or perhaps hard or soft rain, a faint breeze or driving wind. They willingly accept heat and cold as part of their existence, and in any season they always try to welcome the presence of man or animal. Some are carpeted with trees and grass and others are bare, with a cloak of rock and stone. Some mountains are high and mighty and shout their grandeur, while others are more subdued and merely whisper their presence. They stoically endure all the myriad forces of nature and still retain their composure and good nature.

Mountains talk to us in ways we hardly ever acknowledge. It is nothing you can hear but you experience a vivid realization of their strength and constant presence. With man's persistence in modifying the landscape, we can always rely on their relentless immobility. Their lofty perches give birth to the rivers and streams that flow from their bosoms to nourish our land and quench our thirst. Mountains moderate the force of winds and alter their direction. Even as they punctuate the horizon, our global climate recognizes and adjusts to their massive presence. Mountains add dimension and contrast to the topography of the world, and they have affected the course of human history and civilization in incalculable ways. By their massive size and calm beauty, they elevate the spirit of man.

Mountains to me are a source of inspiration and perhaps hope. They are eternal and the values they represent are impervious to time. They resist change in a fast-changing world. They are never bored, because they keep busy adjusting to the vagaries of daily weather and the yearly cycle of the contrasting seasons. They willingly accept your moods and thoughts with no comment. They depend only on themselves for their durability and continued existence. These are values that demand respect, even in man.

Mountains are truly beautiful. You see them as they really are, with no pretense. To enjoy that beauty, you must first rise above or move away from intervening man-made objects like buildings and natural objects like trees. It requires the long view, whether they are near or far. That long view can often change your perspective on life and allow you to understand what is truly important and what is not. Your daily problems and pressures seem to dissipate in the presence of such majesty. You may feel small and almost insignificant. It could even give you new directions to pursue or modify your goals. The least it will do is make you think and afford you a feeling of tranquility.

So please take a moment, or many moments, to look at the sea, the vast plains, the uplands and lowlands, the forests, the lakes and rivers, and the mountains of our world. Look at anything created by nature and realize that you are a vital part of all you survey. Their beauty is part of your heritage, and it is there for you to taste, to help renew your spirit, and expand your soul above and beyond your daily familiarities.

Grandma Myra and I love all of you very much.

Grandpa Gene

To My Grandchild on the Way

February 22, 2004

To my unborn grandchild with love,

You are with your mother developing into a human being as I write this letter to you. The world will still be here whenever you arrive. So please don't rush the process. You will have two loving parents, two terrific brothers, and a full complement of grandparents, aunts, uncles, cousins and more, all waiting anxiously to greet you. All of us want you to be as perfect as you can be. Take all the time you need.

You may find this amusing, but as of this date, February 22, 2004, I don't know whether you are a boy or a girl. It shouldn't really matter much. I love you sight unseen. We all love you sight unseen. The miracle of your birth is making a lot of people ecstatically happy, most particularly your wonderful mother and dad and your two very excited brothers, Steven and Scott. You have affected your new family in a very profound way. Without even stepping over the threshold, you have already entered our hearts and you have found a loving home there forever.

At the moment you are in God's hands, and there is not much for you to think about. However, when the right time does come along, it will be helpful if you are prepared with some basic knowledge of your new venue. After all, you will occupy it for the rest of your life. Your present small location is quiet and peaceful. Please do not expect the real world to be nearly as quiet or quite as peaceful. You may have suspected that fact, because now you are all alone with no one to talk to. But your current voyage will end shortly in a very crowded and busy place, where information and interaction with people are important to your future welfare and happiness.

I have written numerous letters to your wonderful brothers and even one to their future children. So this letter to you is not as strange as it may appear. As my newest grandchild, these letters apply equally to you and to your children as well. Your parents and your brothers will happily share them with you when you are older and you begin to seek your own place in the world. I am writing them for many reasons. I would like my grandchildren to know their grandfather for more than having a meal together or spending a brief visit. All my experiences of a lifetime would be wasted if I didn't take the time and effort to pass on to you a road map of personal behavior that might help make your voyage through life more productive and more satisfying.

It is never easy to know exactly what motivates people. Through these letters I trust you will get to know some of my innermost thoughts and my own motivations. You may learn that I am almost always optimistic and a doer. I try to make things happen, and I have the self-confidence to speak up and make my wishes known. My mind is seldom idle, and I try to keep my body agile. I am constantly aware of my surroundings, and I see beauty and purpose in the simplest things. As a major goal in your life, get to know who you are. Understand what you know and what you don't know — what you can do well and what you cannot do well. Be realistic about your abilities. Always keep growing in knowledge and ability, striving to improve your innate talents. Never hesitate to attempt new things, travel new roads and seek new destinations. Develop the confidence to take risks by carefully weighing the pros and cons of any situation. Oak Tree would have been an unfulfilled dream if your dad and I had not taken a risk. Against much negative advice, we believed in ourselves and the dream of business success came true.

I have been blessed with the time to get to know Steven and Scott. They are wonderful grandsons, and you will be blessed with wonderful brothers. You will enjoy the love of doting parents, devoted to their family and to each other. They will attempt to teach you how to live happily in a world that is not perfect. I know from my experiences that you can always make the future better than the past, if you persist in the present.

Good luck on your journey. I wish you much joy and happiness for a long, healthy and prosperous life.

With much love,

Grandpa Gene

Youth

June 9, 2004

Dear Seven and Scott,

The period when they were young is thought by many adults to have been the best time of their lives. Young people are in generally good health and enjoy high energy levels. We envy their prospects and the time they have to fulfill their hopes and dreams. We admire their youthful appearance and unrestricted appetites. They lack the necessity of making a living and they enjoy more time to play. Their questionable decisions are usually less damaging and more easily forgivable. We often expect them, perhaps unreasonably, to see the world and conduct themselves as adults do. We may even attempt to understand when their choices don't match our expectations.

If you try to tell young people how lucky they are, most of them will give you a look of disbelief. Many of them would like to be older, independent, allowed to solve their own problems with the money and time to indulge in their fantasies. They are in a hurry to grow up and be able to do what they like, when they like. They seek instant maturity, and many young people feel that they have already achieved it. Patience is not usually one of their virtues. Yet there are very few of us mature folk who would not want to be young again, or at least younger than we are.

Returning to an earlier time would give us the opportunity to rethink and redo some choices we made on the road to maturity. We would seek and listen to the advice of our elders more carefully and try to understand the implications of what they were saying. We would attempt to learn more about ourselves, our talents and abilities, and allot more time to develop them. It would help to realize early that disappointments are not the end of the world but may be the key to opening new vistas of accomplishment and growth. The sheer exuberance and the easy friendships of our youth would like to be enjoyed all over again. Finally, after years of independent effort in a competitive world, it might be comforting to be young again under the protective umbrella of a loving family and a caring, active mother and dad.

Looking backward can be a pleasant and rewarding exercise. It does serve to remind us of our roots and how we came to be where we are and who we are. We can remember many of the people we met on our journey and their possible influence on our lives. That could include teachers, relatives, friends, even strangers or almost anyone. Some encounters may have been brief, but they too can leave an impression. Almost any of our past experiences and choices can be reviewed for the results they produced and the lessons they taught us. As we grow older, we learn to adjust more readily to present realities and employ the wisdom we have gained for greater personal fulfillment.

Mature trees grow from little saplings. When all is said and done, let us leave youth to the young people. They deserve their own time to strengthen and spread their roots. Allow them the space to stretch their branches and cast their own influence and shade over the earth. Trees can take root almost anywhere, but they need nourishment and protection. It takes inner strength and a firm trunk to persist against the vagaries of weather, wind, rain, heat and cold, in darkness and light. The only sound they make is the rustle of their leaves, but they have the noble purpose of refreshing the air we breathe and bringing beauty and comfort to an otherwise empty landscape.

I know of no adult tree that would want to be a sapling again. As we grow older, we find that every age has its own rewards and challenges. We learn to enjoy the rewards and accept the challenges with greater calmness and satisfaction. No one of us should want to miss out on the natural succession of human seasons, because to repeat anything takes away its spontaneity and joy of discovery. All any one of us has in our grasp is the present. For that reason alone, the best time in anyone's life is now, because the past is only memory and the future is only hope.

Adam, Steven, and Scott, always try to make the best possible use of today, each and every day.

Grandma Myra and I love you both very much.

Grandpa Gene

Decisions

July 12, 2004

Dear Steven and Scott,

Robert Frost, the famous New England poet, ended one of his most memorable poems with these lines.

"Two roads diverged in a wood, and I -
I took the one less traveled by,
And that has made all the difference."

In previous lines in the same poem:

"Oh, I kept the first for another day!
Yet knowing how way leads on to way,
I doubted if I should ever come back."

You make many choices like this, every day of your lives. Most are simple ones such as what shirt and tie to wear or what to have for lunch. They are easy to make and allow you to change your mind. Others, made less frequently, are more long range and require greater thought and commitment. You should carefully weigh the possible consequences of your choices and their impact on your future. Too much time and activity may have occurred, and it is often quite difficult to retrace your steps and start over. Two examples of important choices are what career to pursue and which college to attend.

You are fortunate in our country to be able to conduct your lives any way you choose without breaking the law or infringing on the rights of others. Making choices is a privilege of our American heritage and our freedoms. That gives you enormous latitude in your pursuit of happiness. It enables you to develop your individuality, to satisfy many personal desires and reach the full potential of your abilities. Making the right choices in large measure can determine the quality of your lives.

Any intelligent decision must be based on reliable information and careful thought. Always fully research your subject, and take the necessary time to think about the path you will choose. Your mistakes will be fewer in number and far less costly. You should make a realistic assessment of your own talent and ability. Will the choices you make and the goals you have set be attainable? Many people choose tasks they are not capable of performing properly and often without sufficient preparation. That is a sure-fire formula for disappointments and possible failure. Therefore, it is wise for you to do your homework, not only in school, but long after you graduate.

There are two other important human traits that alone can very often make the difference between success and failure in any choice you decide. They are not related to your intelligence, or reliable information, careful preparation, proper timing or anything else. One is motivation. Do you have the desire and the will to begin and perform the job you choose to the best of your ability? The other is persistence. Do you have the drive to continue to pursue your goals despite setbacks, obstacles and temporary disappointments? There will be many times in your life that motivation and persistence, almost by themselves, will help bring your tasks to a successful result.

As you mature into manhood, you must assume responsibility for the choices you make. If it is your choice, or your task, it is your result. If any of them do not turn out as planned, you have a choice. You can make every attempt to improve the results. If that is not possible, you can then proceed to some other worthwhile task. Successful people have one thing in common: They get the job done. There are no secrets to their success. They make good choices, and they know what they must do to get the results they seek. If you wish to be successful or even happy, you must make good choices and do everything you can to get the job done.

Grandma Myra and I love you both very much.

Grandpa Gene

Thank You, From Steven 2004

July 21, 2004

Dear Grandpa,

For many years now you've been writing me wonderful letters.
I never really took the chance to thank you for sharing your
endless wisdom and the love you possess. I can't tell you enough
how much I appreciate all you've done. These letters filled with
your experience will carry me through my life and lead me to
success. Your wisdom isn't all I need to succeed. You taught
me that self-confidence is also a necessary component to my
everyday life. I learned from you that to enrich my everyday life
and my adult life I must try to be curious about different things
(like because you studied piano as a boy, you enjoyed music in
your mature years).

I enjoy rereading all of your letters and receiving all your
powerful knowledge for a second or third time. I am exceedingly
glad you took the time to share your wonderful memories.

Thanks again, Grandpa!

I love you,

Steven

Response to Steven 2004

July 21, 2004

Dear Steven,

You have eloquence beyond your years. Your letter may be short, but it makes a powerful statement about a realistic outlook that is unusual in one so young. You have a keen understanding of the true values that make up a well rounded life. At the age of 13 you already know, well before most of your peers, the basics of a happy and successful future.

While I have always been proud to be your grandpa, I am even more proud to call you my grandson. Grandma Myra and I wish you a long, healthy and happy life. We both love you very much.

Love,
Grandpa Gene

From Scott 2004

July 21, 2004

Dear Grandpa,

Over the years I have quietly taken in your insightful wisdom
of the world, and I slowly gathered and formulated ways to apply
your knowledge into my everyday life. I feel, now that I have
listened to what you had to say (you told me to always listen
to people), it would be appropriate for me to give you feedback
on what I have learned from you and what I think about it. If I
could only remember even 10 percent of the knowledge you
have shared with me and incorporate it into my life, my time
spent on Earth would be much more enjoyable. However, I have
remembered much more than 10 percent, and I intend to pass on
your copious insights of life to my children and grandchildren.
I will ensure your letters will be passed and cherished from
generation to generation of Kesselmans.

When you took me back to when you were a young boy such
as myself, I realized how far technological advancements and
ergonomics have gotten us in the world. People in today's day
and age tend to be lazier, because machines can do more things
for them. We sit around watching television instead of playing

games outdoors and creating activities to keep ourselves occupied. We can't appreciate nature for what it is or just look around and enjoy the sights of society. We don't observe people or trees or the sky anymore, because we are always rushing everywhere, to our next appointment, or to pick up your kids, or to the store or the dentist. In our limited free time, however, we don't enjoy the simple pleasures of the world. We will watch some mindless reality TV show or shop for materialistic items. We don't know what sentimental value is anymore, and we have no concept of real beauty. Sometimes we just have to kick back and hold onto what is genuine and meaningful, and we must always appreciate family and friends.

With your eloquence, you have also told me the importance of enjoying my youth. Without a strong childhood and firm social roots, we have nowhere to spring from when we go off into the world on our own. Also, your youth is the time of your life with the most freedom, and choices are made without remorse. Childhood is the peaceful innocence of happiness. By that I am referring to a simple greed leniency adults give to children. When adults spend money on themselves, frivolously throw cash away, they are noted as greedy and selfish. However, children can do this without seeming selfish.

You have also explained to me how motivation and persistence are the two key human traits that can influence decisions we make in our lifetime. We judge if we want to work to accomplish something, and we try to see if we have the continuous drive to work towards our goals to back up the decisions we make. If we make impulsive choices, which we often tend to do as a first reaction, we may be surprised or let down later realizing that we can't accomplish the task or it isn't worth it. Now that you have taught me to carefully plan out the path I take in life, I can be more prepared with my future and more secure with myself. Although, once in a while, when I come to a fork in the road, I'll have to take it. I need to embrace life sometimes and just enjoy that I am here.

I would like to conclude my letter to you with a thought from the book I am reading, "Jasmine." In the book, an Indian woman is living in Iowa, and she adopted a Chinese boy, Du, with her American boyfriend (they aren't officially married). Du is trying to become completely American too fast instead of holding onto his roots. His mother believes that it is important to always hold on to your roots no matter where they come from and you incorporate your traditions and foreign lifestyle into your everyday activities in America. This is what being American is about, and I am glad you have passed down your traditions and past to me so I can hold on to my roots and embrace them.

Thank you for everything.

Love,
Scott

Response to Scott 2004

July 21, 2004

Dear Scott,

Your letter to me is one of the most beautiful letters of any kind
that I have ever read. Certainly no ordinary young teenager
has the skill and insight that you exhibit in this letter. You have
demonstrated more maturity, sensitivity and literary ability than
most people your age and even years older.

As a writer myself, I know the time and immense effort you
took to put those words to paper. Nothing this good can be
done hastily. What you have accomplished takes patience, clear
thinking and an unusual ability to organize ideas. You have
developed the rare skill to communicate, not only verbally, as I
know, but visually with the written word. These are formidable
assets to have as you begin your journey.

Grandma Myra and I are truly proud of you as a man and
particularly as our grandson. We both love very much.

Grandpa Gene

Long Road of Success

August 10, 2004

Dear Steven and Scott,

When I look over the long range of my life, 80-plus years, I am amazed at the all the things that I have done, all the places I have visited and all the people I have met and known, many only briefly. I can go backward to each decade in my mind and visualize the scenes and the mood of the times. I am the sole observer of a silent moving screen that seems to project all the activity but none of the emotions and anxieties that were undoubtedly very real at the time. During this sterile exercise in nostalgia, I often get the feeling that all those events just unfolded by themselves, that I was not involved and had no control over the results. Of course, that cannot be possible, because they are very real to me, and I am able to remember them vividly.

I also remember just as vividly that as a young boy I often had the lonely feeling of being inadequate and unfulfilled. I looked up to almost everyone else, because I was under the impression that they knew many of the secrets of living that I didn't know. I felt that most other people were in many ways happier than I was, didn't have as many problems as I had or in some way had their lives all neatly put together. It wasn't until years later I concluded that what I had done was transfer a normal reverence for my much older three brothers to include many of my peers and the public in general. I actually thought of myself as everyone's kid brother. The only basic confidence I had was in my perceived above-normal intelligence, an ability to learn quickly and a good memory. These may seem like a good place to start a life, but that feeling of being just a junior often caused me to second guess my own thinking and my own activities. I could not enjoy anything like a normal process of growing up, and that early era became a rocky road and a time of stress for me.

For instance, high school was not a particularly happy time in my life. I found close, friendly relationships somewhat difficult to establish and maintain, and I joined few, if any, extracurricular activities. I was not comfortable in the mainstream of school activities. In my local neighborhood, if the boys decided to play touch football in the street, that is what I played with them. I was part of the group but not really in it, and I was considered the quiet intellectual. I felt that opinion was not flattering. What saved me from total despair was a youthful optimism in the future, a curious mind and an awareness of my strengths. These blessings later became the seeds for a personal revival.

My life was to change radically in every way with my enlistment in the Air Force. The military world I entered became one of excitement, purpose and camaraderie. It was with the rigorous flight training coupled with my relatively easy adaptation to military life during World War II that I began to mold a new perspective toward myself and others. It allowed me to interact with and observe, almost clinically, an enormous kaleidoscope of disparate people. They were privates to generals in 11 Air Force bases in the U.S. and Asia, fellow Americans from every corner of the land and ordinary folks from three war-ravaged countries. I listened to their conversation, observed their body language and compared their actions. This human textbook gave me a fascinating insight into the effectiveness of varying personalities, and the courage to begin to examine my own. It opened my eyes to an honest appraisal of my own true self-worth for the very first time. Simply put, I was gaining a strong measure of self-respect that changed my life forever, not overnight, but certainly over time.

I am a long way now from being the kid brother to three older brothers and a caring mom and dad. There is no one person I can truly thank for my transformation. Perhaps I should thank the hundreds, or even thousands, of people I crossed paths with during the war and the years after for allowing me to realize who I really am. Those comparisons with others gave me the courage to look inwardly beyond the restricting inferiority complex, the false envy of others and the paralyzing shyness. Everyone has the ability to be the person they want to be if they would only have the courage to use their minds to think, their legs to move and attempt worthwhile goals, and their arms to hug someone and help those who need help.

Grandma Myra and I love you both very much.

Grandpa Gene

Making It Happen

August 25, 2004

Dear Adam, Steven and Scott,

There are hundreds of little things we do daily to smooth over the rough spots we find on the road of life. We generally learn to do them as a way to save time, avoid inconvenience or disappointment, or to insure our health and well being. These are things like calling ahead to verify reservations or appointments, gassing the car before any bad weather, taking a jacket to the movies in summer or using the restroom before leaving a location. Many of them are either plain common sense or habits that require no further thought. However, there are others that are the result of lessons we have learned the hard way. Let me illustrate just one of these with a short story.

Some years ago, Uncle David submitted an application with supporting documents for admittance to the Rutgers University Graduate School of Business. It was mailed in the fall for a decision to be made by the following May. He had already earned a bachelor's degree in mathematics from Wagner College, and he was seeking a master's degree in accounting. The purpose was to upgrade his job opportunities in a field that was more in demand at that time. Therefore, getting into Rutgers was crucial to his plans and his dreams for the future.

In that year, the months of October and November came and went, as did December, New Year's Eve and the early days of January. At the end of January, it was urgently suggested to Uncle David that he go to the admittance office to see if his application had been received and inquire into status of the admittance procedure. He felt that it was unnecessary and a waste of time. After all, they know their business and his visit would just annoy them. In fact, it might even jeopardize his chances for admittance. Well, I am older, supposedly wiser and his father, and over a period of some weeks I pressed my case. He finally agreed to go, and he made his visit to the Rutgers University admissions office one morning in the middle of February. The decision month of May was just three months away.

He told the young clerk, who was alone in the office, the purpose of his visit. She then began looking into the usual files for his application, but it was not there. She could not find it in any other file or even the dean's office. If there was no application, there was no possible way he could be admitted to college. As David related it later, it was a very tense time, embarrassing for her and with his whole future on the line for him.

While they stood there possibly wondering what to do next, the dean of admissions walked in. He listened to their problem and both of them began to search. Well, after a while and a few very proper expletives, the application was finally found, probably in a most unlikely location. Neither one could understand how it got there. Any office clerk or executive working with the volume of paper necessary in today's business world can easily misfile or misdirect important documents. The dean, in a friendly gesture, invited David into his office for a chat, carrying the newly found documents.

Interviews with applicants are not part of the of admissions process. In this case, David was there, the dean was there and they had just spent a few moments together in a shared experience. They had a pleasant informal chat for about 15 minutes about David's background and future goals, and he left the office. In May, Uncle David received a letter advising him that he was admitted to the Rutgers University Graduate School of Business. I later discovered that only about 20 percent of the total who apply are accepted. David's fateful visit saved his future. There is a fundamental lesson in this story that I had learned years before to my everlasting benefit, and now Uncle David's.

Leave nothing to chance. Whenever your personal interests or welfare are involved, it serves no useful purpose to be timid. First, allow a proper amount of time to elapse. Then in a polite but firm manner start your inquiries until you get an answer. You should never depend totally on anyone else to do the right thing in your behalf. Other people have their own personal priorities, which may not be the same as yours.

That is true for any office, government or otherwise, any individual you may have business with, your lawyer, accountant, any adviser, a friend, your boss, a relative, anyone. Always remember that only you alone are your own best advocate to protect and promote your own best interests. In doing so, and this is a very important point, you will very often find that you are treated with greater respect and even with some admiration.

Grandma Myra and I love all three of you very much.

Grandpa Gene

Learning Goes Both Ways

September 7, 2004

Dear Steven,

I finally saw both films you gave me on Everest. Grandma was out for the afternoon, and I had the chance to play them. They are both different and each one is fascinating. I will look at them many times again. I want to thank you for thinking of me and allowing me to enjoy a part of the world that I have dreamt about for a very long time.

I don't want you to think that you only learn things from me. I also learn from you. When you make a bright comment or tell me some of your observations of the world around you, I hear you. Your perspective on life is just as important as mine, often somewhat fresher. I fully appreciate who you are, and I love who you are. I am very proud of both you and Scott.

Grandpa Gene

Our World, Introduction

September 9, 2004

Dear Billy,

The letter that follows is a good one for you to sit down and discuss with the boys. It may be a subject they think about, perhaps worry about and don't talk about. This letter puts today's world into proper perspective, what with Iraq and terrorism and other evils. It is hopeful and reassuring and a discussion between their father and them will make them feel better. Make separate copies for each of them so they and you can read it and talk about it together. It would be interesting for you to hear what they have to say.

Dad

Our World

September 9, 2004

Dear Adam, Steven and Scott,

I often wonder, as you may wonder, about what kind of a world we are living in. As you study the past as far back as you care to go, it seems that the old days were full of strife, power struggles, mindless wars, ideas, and ideologies of good and bad fighting each other. The pages of history are replete with men and nations using any means possible, including religion, to gain control, to exercise power over others, and to exploit the minds and efforts of the weak and the vulnerable.

In the modern era there was Napoleon, Kaiser Wilhelm, Hitler, the Czar, communism, fascism, religious extremists, dictators and militarists of all kinds. Today, there are the religious fanatics, who use indiscriminate terror and suicide missions to destroy and kill. With all this chaos, past and present, what are we to conclude about the future of mankind? Will there ever be total peace and complete harmony between men and nations? If peaceful coexistence is difficult to achieve among many families, why should we expect it among many larger groups?

So it seems that every age had its bullies, and we have ours.

These tyrants all have their day in the sun and strut the earth with seeming invincibility. They cause untold misery and suffering and deny the world of the imaginative creativity of the human mind. When you take everything from people, even their dignity, and give little or nothing in return, these power-hungry leaders sow the seeds of their own destruction. Sooner or later, the downtrodden and exploited rise up and throw off their oppressive yoke. Even terrorism, our new tyrant, will someday emulate the fate of their predecessors. Their sun will finally set. Their day will end and they will be no more.

With all that in mind, how are you able to study the past and use it to enrich our own lives? If you listen carefully, tucked in among all this chaos, you can hear the voices of reason, creativity, democratic ideals, cooperative effort and common humanity. As a younger man I became intrigued with the creative minds that graced the pages of history, like Aristotle, Socrates, Newton, Galileo, Shakespeare, Michelangelo, Vermeer, Vivaldi, Franklin, Beethoven and hundreds of others. The list is long, and these are the names I choose to remember and enjoy, the thinkers and creators of any age. Many of them lived in a time of hardship and disbelief, and we should honor their perseverance as well as their contributions to human thought, the arts and the sciences. Each one left the world far richer than he found it.

Their counterparts have existed in the modern era, and there are countless others who walk among us today. Times may change, but men and their dreams do not. I am thinking of Einstein, Edison, O'Neil, Hemingway, Picasso, Salk, Gershwin and thousands more. All of us enjoy their music, see their art, read their literature, and live enriched and longer lives with the fruits of their inventions. School may teach you how to think and learn but not necessarily how to live. That depends on you and how you choose to spend your time.

Happiness is learning and doing worthwhile tasks — in other words, being creative. You don't have to write a book or invent something. You can be creative by continuing to develop the talents you were born with in conjunction with an expanding range of new interests. I can enjoy a walk or a bench in the park, a visit to a museum, attending a concert, taking a trip, having a quiet conversation with someone, studying an interesting subject like Nepal or composing a letter to my grandsons. I want to look around every corner and keep my mind busy with new scenes and fresh ideas. My curiosity is endless. Your grandpa can never grow old.

Well within your lifetime, and you are 13 and almost 15, the world has changed dramatically, and that change will accelerate in the years ahead. The new tyrants are going to have a harder time spreading their poison and for many reasons. First of all, free men are not easily swayed by the voices of evil, and more of the world is free. Also, it is more difficult to isolate and conceal the truth with the almost instant exposure of events and information. We can communicate faster and exchange our ideas and knowledge to fuel the minds of the curious and the creators. Vast amounts of information can easily be stored and easily retrieved, enabling free minds to be free to create and accumulate more useful information. Finally, constant new technology will promote the more productive use of time and effort and speed the pace of research.

Today, in your lifespan, history is on our side, and you and I know who is winning. Grandma Myra and I love each of our three wonderful grandsons very much.

Grandpa Gene

Meeting People

September 25, 2004

Dear Adam, Steven and Scott,

Have you ever watched a passing crowd on a busy street corner
or passengers exiting an airplane? I have often stood there
observing them and wondered where everyone is going, what
kind of work they do and what kind of lives they lead? Each one
projects a unique image, a contrasting parade of dress, dreams,
gender and age. The buzz of active humanity rises quickly, and
then in moments begins to fade. The area slowly empties and
awaits the next traffic light change or the arrival of another
airplane. It's like an ocean wave that roars hungrily to shore and
dissipates in a whisper at the shoreline.

We tend to think of all these people as somebody else, as
strangers. In reality they are people, just like you and I. They are
part of our family and we are part of theirs. We are fellow human
beings, and we are all traveling on the same road. All of them
have hopes and goals and problems and friends. Like us, they want
to be loved, understood, believed, appreciated and all those other
wonderful things that can make a life worthwhile. Every one
of them, including you and I, crave recognition as an individual.

As you go through the business of living your lives, you will be meeting and talking to people of all kinds. They will be the very same people who walk by you and I wherever we are, in school, on the job or just traveling. Only now, when you begin to meet them face to face, they become individuals, shedding their anonymity and exposing their thoughts and ideas. Anyone I have ever met in my life, and there must be thousands, has been interesting in some manner and unlike anyone else. Each one has his own personal story and is eager to tell it if you are just willing to listen. They all have new knowledge, new information, even life experiences that could give you new insights into your own life.

Meeting someone for the first time is like opening a new book. It is exciting because you are about to learn something new. If you wish, you can talk to the book. It just won't talk back. You cannot impress a book or ask a question and expect a reply. You give nothing to a book; it gives to you. A conversation with someone is more proactive, because you must think and react spontaneously. You are listening to a distinctive human voice with intonation, cadence and emphasis. This human "book" breathes and thinks, with expressive facial and hand gestures and body language. You can ask questions, offer comments and expect a response.

You should take advantage of any opportunity to meet someone new. It is not always necessary to wait to be introduced. I have walked up to almost anyone I would like to meet, or just acknowledge, and made a comment or introduced myself on any reasonable pretext. It may be a classmate, a teacher, a fellow traveler or anyone in a shared experience, like a neighbor. I have found that my new acquaintance is often flattered and delighted by the attention and recognition he is being given.

A pleasant conversation is one of the singular joys in life. It costs absolutely nothing and can be enjoyed with anyone, anywhere. Even a short greeting such as, "Hello," or, "How are you today?" or a friendly smile to anyone in particular, is enough to make someone's day or a new friend. As you move out into our frantic world, you will find that life's many pleasures are usually the simpler ones, and they are often the most rewarding.

Grandma Myra and I love each of you very much.

Grandpa Gene

Humor

October 2, 2004

Dear Adam, Steven and Scott,

I know very few people who do not enjoy a good joke. It can turn a group of strangers into friends in an instant. A humorist is always a welcome guest anywhere. However, humor is much more than just a series of jokes. It's like looking at a house upside-down. It looks funny, but it is still a house. Humor is only a different way of looking at a situation, whether we see it upside-down, convoluted or twisted. The situation has not changed, only our perception of it. In our daily lives, very often a fresh humorous look can put many things into their true perspective.

We can often take some measure of a person by how they handle humor. All of us have different ideas of what we believe is funny. Some people are embarrassed, annoyed, cynical or even unsure. It takes a level of maturity, at any age, to appreciate and use humor in an honest and acceptable manner. If we are in a serious mood or feel ill, humor in any form may not be on our agenda that day. Certainly all of us have enjoyed the fun and frolic at a party where humor can be exhibited in all its forms. Formal jokes, funny comments, even ribald action, can transform quiet formality into a memorable occasion of either fun or annoyance. Like beauty to the eye, humor is in the mind of the beholder.

Humor can often distract us from the real issues. It can be used as a smoke screen to hide the truth, cover embarrassment or shield motives. You may ask someone a serious question and get a humorous answer instead. Politicians and others are very adept at this type of deception. It can be used to postpone serious discussions or a necessary course of action. Humor, therefore, can often be a barometer into someone's true intentions. In many ways someone's use of humor, either offering it or reacting to it, can reveal the kind of person they really are. If you look carefully, it can be a window into an individual's personality, his sensibilities and, of course, his sense of humor. It may even reveal, in some manner, his perspective on life.

Humor can also be an effective weapon in calming the playing field in any controversy, because it provides a momentary basis for a common understanding. All of us have been in situations where a little humor changed the dynamics between opposing parties, and everyone enjoyed a good laugh together.

Comedians and humorists make a living drawing attention to their real-life trials and tribulations. We laugh with them because they mirror our lives and allow us to see ourselves in a fresh light. They are a very uptight group of people, which may have prompted them becoming comedians in the first place. Humor is a way they ease the pressures of their daily lives. Humor is the catalyst that can help each of us keep our feet on the ground and our lives in perspective. It prevents us from taking ourselves too seriously.

The next time you get caught in a downpour without an umbrella or spill a glass of water in a restaurant, you can either laugh or cry. I'll let you decide which is best. As you make your way in the world, please take a little time periodically and remember that upside-down house.

I love each one of you very much.

Grandpa Gene

War and the Unexpected

October 22, 2004

Dear Steven, Adam and Scott,

There are many circumstances that will occur during our lives that we are unprepared for. They often come as a complete surprise, and we have to be able to adjust quickly to the new set of realities. The cause can be as varied as a household water line break to the sudden loss of your job. Whatever it may be, we must begin seeking solutions with little delay. We do not often have the luxury of time. Let me relate a personal story of one such happening.

Less than 18 months after I was commissioned an officer in the Air Force, I was ordered to be deputy commander of a 1,200-man squadron stationed in the west area of the Alamogordo Army Air Force base in New Mexico. It was just after the end of hostilities in Europe, and our base was a staging area for Air Force combat units returning to the U.S. Some were to be redeployed to the war in Asia.

I was 24 at the time, a first lieutenant trained as an aerial navigator and thrust into a job for which I had absolutely no experience or training. My commanding officer was a major, a charming man and former banker. We also had a sergeant assistant, newly assigned only five days before me. He quickly informed me of our unusual situation. The major was frequently indisposed. He drank too much. We both soon agreed that the actual responsibility for commanding the squadron was mine by default.

That first day sitting in my small bare office at headquarters close to the flight line was an eye-opening experience. All the major wished to discuss, when he finally arrived, was his life as a civilian and little else. The sergeant filled me in on some of the morale, discipline and other problems that he had observed. I knew that somehow I had to begin carrying my own weight, and soon. I also realized that I could not allow myself, in any way, to appear to be indecisive or uncertain, even to him. There were no job description manuals to tell me how to manage 1,200 men.

I remember going to my window late that morning and staring out at the hazy Sacramento Mountain Range running north and south, filling the horizon nine miles east of the base. I stood there for many minutes in deep thought, tinged with a little despair. The sun, filtering through flimsy curtain clouds, made the lofty treeless rock mass appear indistinct and surreal. Two bombers were roaring down the parallel runways, taking off for bombing exercises up the valley. Then I turned, left my small office and began a slow, thought-filled walk around the outside of the headquarters shack. The base had been erected hurriedly with spit, lumber and help from the British only two years before. I had asked the sergeant not to disturb me until I returned.

I began to make some progress only when I directed my thoughts away from myself and my problems to what could be on the minds of the men. They probably knew all about the major and his drinking. At the same time, they must surely be wondering what the "new boy in town" was like and speculating what changes he was likely to make. What could I do to dispel their anxieties and perhaps some of my own? I had to make some kind of defining move quickly. It then occurred to me that the mess hall was the one place where they gathered in a large group at essentially the same time. That opportunity was just what I was looking for.

That evening the sergeant and I went the mess hall to see, be seen and have a meal with the men. Our visit would also show them our interest in their welfare right at the outset. The sergeant had remarked that this approach was a first for him, but he liked the idea. We entered the hall about 20 minutes after the start of mess, when the hall had begun to fill. We walked slowly along the food line and then out among the tables. I introduced myself and the sergeant, and we exchanged brief small talk and asked simple questions. The men seemed to range in age from the late teens to around 32–34. I made sure we covered the entire hall and then doubled back as it slowly cleared and filled again.

I had learned a great deal from their comments and answers. It was truly an invaluable hour plus, and we seemed to have accomplished even more than I could have expected. We then waited our turn in the food line, picked up our meal and ate in a small alcove near the kitchen. Years later, I was reading a popular business management book that contained a chapter entitled "Managing by Walking Around." It appeared that I had done just that by instinct, long before, as young Air Force officer.

After we had eaten, I asked the sergeant to remain and discuss the situation we faced. At 35, he had spent 14 years in the military. I listened very attentively, soaking up his experience and applying it to some tentative plans. I needed more. The next day, I requested a meeting with the commanding officer of the east area, and he agreed to see me the following morning. His responsibilities were the same as my CO. The east and west areas were over two miles apart on opposite sides of the runways, connected only through the main base at the end of the runways, three miles to the south. It was a combat zone layout, designed to minimize any enemy bombing damage. That was certainly not necessary in mainland United States.

The major greeted me cordially, and from the way he talked I knew he realized my predicament, CO and all. He was career military and somewhere under 40. We talked about the war and about our respective jobs. Then I began asking him some very specific questions. That got him rolling, and he gave me some solid basics on military administration mixed with some personal experience and even some base gossip: 65 very informative minutes passed quickly. I stood up, thanked him for his time, saluted and left. In only two days I was off to a running start.

With 1,200 men, you can imagine the variety of issues, many personal, that had to be considered. I asked the sergeant to handle the more routine ones. Within a day, we had put up a general set of rules and regulations on the bulletin board and in the barracks that were clear and concise. I also made myself available to anyone in the squadron who wanted to see me but only at posted designated times. That was done to cut down on continuous, all-day traffic. In every case, I always tried to be fair and equal, keeping in mind the welfare of the men and the requirements of our mission. As you might guess, I did some hand holding and at times felt like a mother hen. It came with the territory, and I took it seriously. There were no how-to manuals for that either.

In the middle of all this, I had one interesting assignment that bears mentioning. As a base officer, it became my turn to serve as

"Officer of the Day," It was actually overnight duty as the officer in charge of the entire Air Force base, east, west and main areas. The military purpose was to have an officer awake and available to deal quickly with nighttime emergencies. These could include ground accidents of all kinds, plane crashes, fires, power failures, security breaches and the like. With over 4,000 men stationed at the base, the potential for trouble can be stressful. During the night, the phone ring was usually not a social call. I did resolve a moderate number of problems, two quite involved but nothing that I considered major.

It was a long night, and I was pleased to see the sergeant major arrive early. However, I could only be relieved from duty by another officer, and 20 minutes later the deputy base commander came in. We chatted for a few moments about one incident he was aware of. I can't recall if there was another Officer of the Day for day duty as well. Then, I turned my report over to the sergeant, and I left to get some sleep. It is this kind of responsibility that can mature any young man quickly.

As the weeks wore on, I felt comfortable in my new role. I called the major in the east area only twice for additional information. I attended regular staff meetings at base headquarters, including one with the visiting major general commanding the 2nd Air Force, of which we were a part. From time to time, I would leave my office and walk around the squadron area and the flight line, poking unannounced into various locations. My attitude was friendly, yet inquisitive, and it gave me a sense of their daily activities and the state of their morale. Our steadily improving performance ratings, posted periodically by the base inspectors, were evidence that things were progressing very well.

Grandpa Gene and Myra — Alamagordo, New Mexico, 1944.

Grandpa Gene about town while stationed in Japan.

Alamagordo, New Mexico, 1944.

A quiet moment off duty in Japan, 1945.

August and September came and went. The war with Japan was already over. In early October, I received orders transferring me to the headquarters of the Pacific Air Command, U.S. Army (PACUSA) at Fort McKinley, Manila, Philippine Islands. I was ready to move on. My job was no longer a challenge.

I felt that I had achieved a high measure of success, and that I had earned the respect of most of the men. I posted a farewell notice, thanked everyone for their cooperation and wished them all good luck. That period of my military life, like all the others, was a learning experience of immeasurable dimensions. When I said my goodbye to the major, he kindly thanked me for my efforts. I respected his rank, and I had always taken the time to keep him fully informed of my activities. Later, I learned that he gave me an excellent rating on my proficiency report. The day I left, the sergeant saluted me, shook my hand and then, to my surprise, gave me a bear hug. The hug was not exactly Army protocol.

I had been given a job to do, and I was expected to do it to the best of my ability. That can happen just as well in civilian life as in the military. You have only one choice in any situation. If you have no idea what to do, you must find out fast. From my first day as an aviation cadet in aerial navigation school, failure of any kind was just not acceptable.

There was only one reply, and one only, that our instructors would accept for any foul up, academic or otherwise, totally regardless of fault or circumstances. It was just three words. "No excuse, sir." It had to be shouted out loud, and often could be heard a block away. If it wasn't loud enough to suit the instructor, we were ordered to shout it again.

In eight months of training in navigation school, that noisy answer could be heard from any one of the 400 men in our cadet class almost daily. About 30 percent of the class eventually washed out before graduation. Was it hazing? Yes! Was it intimidation? Yes! However, it did one thing that I would never forget. It instilled in me a can-do attitude and a can-do frame of mind that has remained with me and persisted all my life. Failure is never an option. "No excuse, sir," still resounds in my brain today.

My wonderful grandchildren, Adam, Steven and Scott, remember this for always. Never make excuses. Just do it.

Grandma Myra and I love you each one of you very much,

Grandpa Gene

The Voyage

November 27, 2004

Dear Adam, Steven and Scott,

Over the past four years, I have probably sent you over 40 letters. My major purpose, among many others, was to help make the long journey ahead of you easier and more successful. The wisdom that we seniors collect as we travel through life is still learned by every newcomer for themselves. It will be that way for you and your children and theirs. If all of us were born wise and mature with a predictable and certain future, what incentive would there be in pursuing the rest of our lives? All the fun of discovery would be gone.

The joy of life is in the uncertainty. There is no mental GPS navigation system to insure that you will reach your desired destination. However, the less you think you know about the future, the more exciting are your efforts to make it a happy and successful one. The suspense in not knowing gives your life the spontaneity and the motivation to persevere. All you can do on the road is the best you know how. Just remember that true happiness and peace of mind is not the destination: They are really intended to be part of the trip itself.

We wish you, "Bon Voyage!"

Grandma Myra and I love all of you very much.

Grandpa Gene

Wisdom

December 17, 2004

Dear Adam, Steven and Scott,

Many of the ideas in this letter I have mentioned in previous letters. However, I do not believe that I ever connected them specifically to the concept of wisdom. This explanation should impress on your young minds that wisdom is available to you in a simple method that has been a habit with me for most of my life. Knowing each of you as I do, you may be doing this instinctively now on your own. The point for you is to make this method a constant, deliberate effort and not an infrequent one.

It was Ben Franklin who said that early to bed, early to rise makes a man healthy, wealthy and wise. When is it possible to realize that you have reached that desirable goal? Both health and wealth can be measured and defined easily. For the first one, you visit the doctor and for the other, you add up your assets. That leaves wisdom, and how do you measure that? What is wisdom anyway? It cannot be taught. There is no academic course labeled Wisdom 101 in any college. How can you actually become a wiser human being? Let's explore this interesting question together.

You should realize that some wisdom is present in all of us at any age. In its simplest form, wisdom is just plain common sense. If I had to make any distinction between the two, I would say that common sense is innate. Wisdom, on the other hand, is accumulated over a lifetime. Simply put, you are born with the first, and you learn the second. You cannot honestly assume that everyone is equally endowed with common sense or the ability to acquire wisdom. It depends totally on the nature of your intellect and who you are as an individual.

Wisdom begins to develop when thought and a curious mind start to compare patterns of cause and effect in both yourself and as observed in others. Let me explain. You embark on a course of action, any one of thousands you do in a lifetime. That is the cause, as in causing something to happen. It can be as simple as preparing a meal to choosing the girl you will marry. It may turn out to be either successful or unsuccessful. That is the effect or the result. Depending on the cause or action, short or long term, it may take minutes, hours, months or even years to determine any outcome. If it is successful, then you either planned properly or were very lucky or both. It really makes no difference. Your plans worked out, and that is all that matters at the moment.

Now suppose your plans do not work out. You are either partially or totally unsuccessful. The poet Robert Burns wrote that the best laid plans of mice and men often go astray. Naturally, the result was not what you expected, and you are disappointed and even unhappy. Do not waste your time fretting or denying the truth. Avoid becoming emotionally attached to a disappointing project or blaming someone else for the outcome. These will serve no useful purpose. Instead, this is the time at which a thinking and a curious mind goes to work to discover some of the reasons and even some possible solutions. Try to understand and discover why your cause or action either failed or is in jeopardy. Wisdom does not come easily; it must be earned the hard way.

That is the major point of this letter. It is your disappointments, your failures and mistakes that hold the key to making you a wiser person. That lifelong process of disappointment and continual analysis is the source of your growing wisdom. Success is not the best teacher and most particularly in your early years. It could give you a false sense of security and then leaves you emotionally vulnerable to the inevitable disappointments that, sooner or later, happen to everyone. You must be wise enough to admit and then learn from your mistakes, all of them, and try not to repeat them. If you realize that important premise, you will be on your way to a more rewarding and more productive life. You will then begin to become a much wiser individual and more capable of making wiser choices.

Grandma Myra and I love each one of you very much.

Grandpa Gene

P.S. I have known and met many people who almost never admit to making a mistake, even to themselves. They are classic cases of stubbornness and self-denial. You and I now realize that personal experience can be the greatest teacher of all because it is difficult to forget what you have lived through. Learning from experience (your own personal classroom) is the greatest teacher of all, and it never stops.

GG

Boredom

January 25, 2005

Dear Adam, Steven and Scott,

In all my letters to you, I have always tried to stress positive attributes. Among them were curiosity, developing your basic talents and learning something from every experience. I have never mentioned a situation that affects every one of us, young and old, at one time or another. It is called boredom — just common everyday boredom.

Boredom can set in, even though you may be surrounded by any number of people. Boredom recognizes neither time nor place. It can be triggered by a combination of tiredness, temporary disappointment, apathy, lost interest and even illness. In today's world everyone seems to be so busy. We literally do not have the time to set aside any substantial time to think. We go from activity to activity, trying to fill up every minute of every day. It is almost embarrassing to be idle, or more to the truth, to be seen as idle.

We often look for things to do. Plain quiet contemplation with no television, radio or other disturbance is not considered doing something. Any idle time we do have, we tend to worry about not having something to do. Few people admit to being bored, and, therefore, the subject is rarely ever discussed. They may say that they have nothing to do, or have no plans, but that may just be a more comfortable way of expressing it.

Suppose you are sitting quietly in a chair doing nothing at all, perhaps just looking out the window. You take for granted that your heart is working — that all your internal organs and cells are working in quiet harmony to sustain your waking experience. Fortunately, that is one thing that you never have to think about it. What is your mind doing? You should know that your mind, like your heart, is working also. Boredom is a golden opportunity to coax your mind into some quiet useful purpose — simply to think about something you may never make the time to think about.

You could think about school, friends, your new brother, family, your future, new activities or almost anything at all. Think time is just as important as busy time. I take walks to exercise, of course, but also to think. What do I think about? It could be anything from a recent incident in my life to the tidal wave disaster in Asia. Even when I am alone in the car, my mind wanders in thought. I get ideas about different things I could or should be doing, getting a handle on current problems, my friends, the past, the future. Often, at home, I will turn the TV off just to sit quietly and have a thoughtful conversation with myself. Let us change the name "boredom" to "think time."

I have often that felt that the more intelligent you are, the quicker you can become bored. Your mind understands and absorbs situations and facts quickly and, therefore, you can lose interest just as quickly. True or not, those quiet, and seemingly boring times, can be valuable and rewarding. It can offer a new look at old situations and a greater understanding of who you are and where you are going. Albert Einstein began his first thoughts about the theory of relativity during his daily walk home from his job at the Swiss Patent Office. That walk and think time defined the rest of his life.

Grandma Myra and I love each of you very much.

Grandpa Gene

Reflections of a Senior

April 18, 2005

Dear Scott, Steven and Adam,

We hear a great deal about senior citizens these days. Since they are living longer than their predecessors, they are growing in numbers, making them more visible everywhere. Today's seniors are more active and in many ways more productive. They travel more, engage in sports and exercise programs, and some continue to work. Many of them are just too busy to dwell on the fact that most of their living is behind them.

Personally, I feel lucky and even blessed for all the additional years and the opportunities all that extra time has given me. As I reflect on each of my milestone decades, from age 20 on, I realize that I have never suffered the traumatic anxieties of getting older that can affect many people. Yet, every year of my life has had its quota of joys and disappointments. Uncle Sol, who lived to almost 96, always advised me to just "keep moving." Those two words, to me, meant having a positive attitude and a relentless curiosity and zest for life, regardless of current circumstances.

However, you cannot enjoy the full richness of life at any age without some plan or guideline. It's like taking a trip. First you decide where you want to go, then how to get there and then the activities you wish to enjoy when you arrive. You may read guidebooks to familiarize yourself with the area and seek other information to make the most rewarding use of limited vacation time. Well, your life, every age of it, requires the same consideration. As I reflect, I realize that I have always had travel plans for trips, for life and the destinations I want to reach. The following considerations have made my goals easier to attain and more enjoyable when I arrived.

An active interesting life means thinking and planning ahead. When I have something to look forward to, it gives me hope and purpose. There are more places I want to visit, so I am thinking of my next trip. I am constantly learning a new skill on the computer. My new car includes navigation and satellite radio, giving me more options for fun. I enjoy music, art, scenery, trees, travel and much, much more. My aching back has even surrendered to my decision to return to golf and exercise at a gym. It will continue to discomfort me anyway, as it has for 30 years, but now I have given it a valid reason. I continue to seek the company and/or conversation with people of all ages and genders, to exchange ideas and learn new points of view. It is important for my wellbeing to maintain an active membership in the human family.

Optimism is another secret that has carried me a long way. Every life has its highs and lows. Either one can arrive and affect your life at any time, and neither one lasts forever. I have had my share of both. No setback has ever been allowed to discourage or paralyze me for long. I have learned that hidden within every disappointment is a golden opportunity for greater wisdom and growth. Even today, I am determined to make my future more productive and happier than the past. In my mind, there is no other choice.

Curiosity keeps my days interesting and my intellect active. I have a constant desire to understand the latest technologies; important and relevant world news; and interesting information about people, places and things. For instance, if I am anywhere temporarily, like in a waiting room, I will read anything at hand, talk to almost anyone willing to talk. The world is an interesting place. It happens to be where I live at the moment. I just like to know as much as I can about it.

I can also sit quietly or take a walk, mind my own business and take an inventory of the ideas running through my mind. I turn them over and under and examine them from all sides. It is amazing to me how the alone moments can allow you to discover new insights into your current problems and activities and add productive fuel to your thinking machine.

Good health is also a necessary blessing, since any active and productive life requires high levels of energy. You cannot neglect or abuse your physical being and expect lady luck to keep you fit and healthy forever. If you have any desire to enjoy more years with family and friends and live long enough to witness the fruits of your labors, God and nature absolutely require your constant cooperation.

Seniors, after all, are just like all other people, only older. Our lives, both yours and mine, are just what we choose to make it. As the experiences of life impact each of you, you must rivet your mind and do not delay making personally beneficial responses. As you know, these have been recurring themes in every one of my letters to you. Savor them and read them at least every few years or as often as you like. They will afford you both comfort and reassurance. You will be amazed at how much more pertinent and meaningful they will become with each reading. You will have your favorites, as I do.

Please remember for always that both Grandpa Gene and your dad have traveled this road for a while, and we know and understand. Just like the ocean tides, there is a constant ebb and flow to your life. You must learn to take full control and shape it to your will. You are the only one who can.

Grandma Myra and I love each of you very much,

Grandpa Gene

Father's Day 2006

June 19, 2006

Dear Scott, Steven and Adam

I am blessed with the most wonderful grandsons in the whole world. That makes me the luckiest grandpa in the whole world. I am lucky in other ways in that I have been allowed to see you mature into well-spoken, bright, personable young adults, even little Adam. Each of you shine as a welcoming presence in any group, young or old.

I am proud of you for many reasons, but one stands out. For many years now, I have been able to talk to you as equals, adult to adult. That tells me a lot about your maturity, your realistic outlook, and your ability to understand and utilize new ideas and information. You have read my letters, you have listened to your dad, and your schooling will continue with all the people you meet and the fascinating world around you. For you, learning never stops.

Adam will follow in your path. He will listen and learn from you, as well as his mother and his dad. He is a lucky little boy, as all of us are. Thank you, Adam, for your card, Steven for your PowerPoint card, Scott for your certificate, and Raellen and Billy for your card. It was a wonderful afternoon. I hope we can all enjoy many more Father's Days together.

Love to all of you,

Grandpa Gene

Foundations, Concentration and Dreams

July 1, 2006

Dear Adam, Steven and Scott,

"Twenty years from now you may be more disappointed by what you did not do than what you did. So, release the bow and stern lines, catch the trade winds, and sail away from safe harbors to dream, to explore and to discover." — *Mark Twain*

This quotation embodies the life of Mark Twain. He traveled the world over, writing, lecturing, becoming famous for his wisdom, his insight and humor. He was the Ben Franklin of the 19th century, a man for all seasons and for all ages. It appears that he did most of what he wanted to do, and there would not be much that he could regret in 20 or even 40 years. Only Mark Twain would know the true answer to that.

When you postpone doing something that either you should do or just want to do, you create two scenarios. You will either have to somehow squeeze it into a busy future or you may never to do it at all. In any active life, there are many things that will fall by the wayside. These are both the big and small crumbs of life that may or may not seem overly important to you at the time. Later, even years later, some of them can assume a disproportionate relevance in your mind and perhaps cause feelings of regret.

What can someone with a fertile mind and a zest for life do to be truly happy? In baseball, a third baseman cannot cover second base at the same time. He must confine his expertise and training to doing his best job at third base. Likewise, if there are two or more chairs available for you to sit on, you have to pick one. You can only sit in one chair at a time or be involved in one situation at a time. You have to set priorities, parcel your time and your energies to do initially what must be done effectively each day to carry out that day's responsibilities. The rest is personal fluff and leisure time, which are equally important and necessary for you to enjoy a well-rounded and fulfilling life.

I was young at a different time, with my early years interrupted by wartime. During that period, I had the good fortune to taste the exotic fruit of distant lands. Upon my return I had to hustle to make up for all the years that I had lost. I never made it to Nepal or became a concert pianist. I never became a mountain climber or an explorer to remote places. But I did dream, and over the years, many of my dreams have been realized. One that I am especially proud of is the fact I traveled extensively and took more trips than anyone I know. No one person can ever do it all, but I still try. That effort continues to keep me young in spirit and in mind.

Adam, Steven and Scott, for everything that grows there is a season, and this is your season for preparation. It is the time for you to study the basic tools of your approaching adulthood, to develop your unusual intellectual gifts and to hone your skill at learning. This is also the time for you to begin to know who you are as an individual, to realize what you enjoy doing and what you can do well. As an expanding world unfolds before you, your heart and your mind will dream of the future. Please remember to keep some of your dreaming both practical and attainable or else too many of them may remain just dreams.

Grandma Myra and I love each of you very much.

Grandpa Gene

The Future, From Steven 2006

July 7, 2006

Dear Grandpa and Grandma,

Over the years, you have written Scott and me many letters that instilled strong messages, insights and memories. As I look back and read them again, those same morals and discernments reappear. I cannot tell you enough how much I appreciate these letters you write us. I can read them throughout my entire life and be guided by your savvy. Thanks again, Grandpa.

As I was rereading a few of your letters, one certain motif really intrigued me. I found it interesting to think about the tremendous technological advancements from the time of your childhood to now. I found a quote by Einstein that really got me thinking, "I know not with what weapons World War III will be fought, but World War IV will be fought with sticks and stones." With all of these advancements in weaponry and combat tactics, World War III may cause a catastrophic reverse in science. Will anything be left of the world? Maybe all this development will lead us backwards. It definitely is something to think about, especially with all these recent nuclear threats.

I found one more quote that I felt validates the importance and necessity of your letters. Machiavelli, the Florentine man of politics, once wrote, "Whoever wishes to foresee the future must consult the past; for human events ever resemble those of preceding times. This arises from the fact that they are produced by men who ever have been, and ever shall be, animated by the same passions, and thus they necessarily have the same results." I enjoyed this quote, and if you think about it, your letters are the past that Scott, Adam and I will consult to clear our own paths to the future. Our experiences will match yours, but the three of us will have these letters, which will give us an advantage. You learned the morals and insights the hard way, Grandpa, and now we can continue our lives without too many surprises.

I love you and Grandma very much,

Steven

Perspective, From Scott 2006

July 7, 2006

Dear Grandpa,

Over the past week after reading your letter, I came across two quotes that I thought I should share with you that reminded me of your message. The first of which was from Abraham Lincoln. It went, "And in the end, it's not the years in your life that count. It is the life in your years." This reflects your belief in living life to its fullest and making the most out of your time on earth. A full life, when it's all said and done, is not marked by many years necessarily, but by accomplishing personal goals and filling your time with projects and activities that make you happy.

The second quote came from an English author whom George Bernard Shaw dubbed a "colossal genius," G.K. Chesterton. He claimed that, "An adventure is only an inconvenience rightly considered. An inconvenience is an adventure wrongly considered." This also echoed words that you have passed on to us before, to take whatever life doles out and make the best of it. His statement insinuates that anything in life can be exhilarating and enjoyable if you look at it the right way. I am going to keep this thought with me, and maybe when life throws me the proverbial curve, I can turn it around and hit it out of the park. I hope you enjoyed those quotes; I'll let you know if I see any more interesting ones.

I love you,

Scott

Football and the Crib

July 10, 2006

Dear Scott, Steven and Adam,

In the very beginning, life is uncomplicated and peacefully quiet. The darkness and isolation of the womb is serene, but we learn nothing. Our bodies are slowly being assembled and soon begin to run automatically on their own. In due time, we are born, bare, wet and naïve. Any resemblance to a normal human being requires a vivid imagination.

We begin to breathe air instead of fluid, and immediately our first outside visitors show up uninvited. These strangers squeeze and kiss us, talk baby talk, and make funny faces. We have no idea where we are and make no sense of anything we see and hear. We can get what we want just by crying, which is not very civilized. We can do anything we want, at any time, and someone else cleans it up. The crib is our entire world, small, simple and cozy. This could be the happiest time of our entire lives, but unfortunately, we will not remember any of it.

Soon, we outgrow the crib and begin traveling the long road from dependence to independence. The three of you are in the middle of that trip right now. Look at it this way. Before you can play football, you must train hard, learn plays and scrimmage. Almost too soon, scrimmage is over and the real game begins. You fight for every yard, back and forth, up and down the field, and get roughed up. It is all part of the game, and you play it, even enjoy it, for all you're worth. After four quarters, the game is over. You must have learned something today, and next week is another game. Think of life as an extended football game, and you are now in training camp.

It was always my hope that the letters would assist you to a more mature outlook at an early age. Add in your agile minds, and you could mentally be 30 or 40 years old well before your 20th birthday. I am strongly considering letting you write my letters, and I would just sign them. Then again, I have more free time than any of you. I guess we will leave things as they are for the moment. Both of you are too busy, and Adam has a few years to go before reporting to training camp.

Grandma Myra and I love each of you very much,

Grandpa Gene

Three Themes, Up the River

August 15, 2006

Dear Adam, Steven and Scott,

This is a special letter. It has just three short paragraphs with three different themes. This is a wonderful opportunity for you to discuss them with each other, your dad, a teacher or a friend. You can expand each theme into a flood of parallel ideas. You will have some very interesting discussions and lots of fun too. Please try it.

Grandpa Gene

1. Can you answer this provocative question? Who is the most important person in your life? Is he a friend, family member, a relative, an acquaintance, a teacher or perhaps none of these? It must be someone you know well and deal with every day. In fact, this person is probably so important to you that you could never get very far without him. He would have to be with you all the time, day and night. You would share the same dreams, hear what he hears, see what he sees and think exactly the way he thinks.

He would be close enough to be your alter ego. He could possibly be you, and in truth, he is you. You and you alone are the most important person in your life, since everything you do affects your life in some way. No one else in the entire world has that extraordinary power over your destiny.

2. Think of life as a swift flowing stream. Some people just stare at the water and prefer to remain dry. Life is just too complicated for them. Then there are the insecure, who barely get their feet wet, hesitate for a while and then get out. That pattern keeps repeating itself throughout their lives. The less timid cautiously enter the stream and stay at various depths up to their shoulders. Above that constantly moving level, they remain dry. They are never quite certain of their commitment or resolve or ever realize who they truly are. Finally, there are the intrepid few, adventurous, challenging, who dive in headfirst. They are confident, fully prepared with set goals and the perseverance to achieve them. They immerse themselves fully into the stream of life. If you are ever going to accomplish anything worthwhile, you have to literally get totally wet.

3. Watching a TV show or a football game requires no special skills, only your wakeful attention. You have nothing to do but look, listen and eat peanuts. For many people, being a spectator is their favorite activity. It has one undeniable accomplishment — it fills up time. But it is not happiness. Roosevelt once wrote that (true) happiness is the joy of achievement and the thrill of creative effort.

For the salesman, it means getting an order. Creating a work of art does it for the artist, a novel for the author, a new business for the entrepreneur, a dwelling for the builder. It could be a new recipe for the housewife, study and learning for the student or as simple as improving a skill. It can only be done by people with busy hands, a thinking mind and a passionate heart. Many people spend their whole lives searching for happiness in people, places and things. Yet, it is right there at home within themselves. It is in anything that would not exist unless you create it. Please remember that whatever it is that you do, just do it to the best of your ability.

Love,
Grandpa Gene

194 Just Do It

Just Do It

Dear Steven and Scott,

Grandma Myra and I are enjoying the warm weather here in
Florida. Up north, the cold would keep us too confined. I am
sorry it is cold there, but it is really the way it should be. While
we know that global warming is coming, plants starting to bloom
in February would not be normal. Our present government
keeps denying the obvious signs of changing weather patterns
and is doing very little to combat it. In two years, we will have a
new president and, I hope, a government more responsive to the
realities of our times.

I know that both of you are busy, and that is the way it should
be. In all your activity, be sure that you schedule your time wisely.
I try to do that here. I must find time for golf, reading, computer,
exercise, and more and still fit in other projects like adjusting my
glucose testing equipment, getting the information ready for tax
time on April 15 and so forth. These chores never end and are
personal to each of us. How we choose to live is personal, and it
defines our whole life. If you establish good habits of work now,

they will serve your best interests all your life. I am constantly reminded of the Nike slogan, "Just do it."

Grandma and I miss you both very much. We appreciate your phone calls and enjoy hearing your voices and talking to you.

Remember always, we love you.

Grandpa Gene

College

April 24, 2007

Dear Steven and Scott,

The joy and the responsibility of finding a college and available scholarships belongs to you and not dad or your mother. In the last few months and even the last few years and as late as today, I have spoken to numerous parents and grandparents whose children have decided on a school they will attend and won scholarships. There are not just one or 10 or 20 good colleges, but hundreds. There are thousands of scholarships awarded for just as many reasons and stipulations. My lawyer's daughter is going to a school in California free of charge, all expenses paid. The younger daughter goes to the University of Virginia. State schools generally run much cheaper than private schools, but they are top rated. And any college has to be applied to, but by you alone.

Talk to your guidance counselor at school, not once, but many times. Become his friend, flatter him as to the importance of his job and pick his brains as you know Grandpa would do. This is no time to be shy. Your future is at stake. Talk to teachers — they know something about colleges. Find out what they know. Talk to anyone who might have information you might be able to use. Picking a college is a project, an important one. It's personal homework for yourself. All these people are flattered that you seek their advice. I certainly would be, and remember: Good ideas can come from any source, even a fellow student.

The internet is your best starting source. It can open the whole academic world to you. As Grandpa always says, "If you don't ask, you don't get." Remember, this is your future, and it starts right now and right here. Your parents give you food, clothing, shelter, love and guidance. You yourself have to take on the world and find your own road to your future. That means you finding your own college and applying and seeking scholarships. They are out there like apples on a tree, ready for plucking. Someone is going to get them, and it might as well be you. Both of you have so much to offer, but you must believe in yourself and others will believe in you.

As I once wrote to you, life is a swift flowing stream. Jump in, get totally wet. As it flows, the stream widens and grows bigger, the shores become wider apart and soon it becomes a delta with many tributaries that flow majestically to the wide exciting ocean. That's the world and that's life, and if you don't jump in now, you remain back at the narrow headwaters. Just watch the water flow and you go nowhere.

So go to it, get busy and make your own opportunities. Grandma Myra and I know you can do it. Do and learn; do and learn. We love you both very much, we wish you every success, we will watch you through good days and bad, and you will persist. We believe in you.

Love,
Grandpa Gene

Power in You

April 24, 2007

Just a follow up note:

You yourself are more important than the school you attend. Yes, it must be well rated; yes, it must excel in the field you choose; yes, it must have all the amenities for research, study, scholarship, sports and social activities. There are hundreds of good schools of all sizes and many I have never heard of that are great. But the school you choose is only a means to an end and not an end in itself, and that end depends solely on you. You are more important than the school.

Education, college, is just a tool — a hammer to hit the nail; a car for transportation; a computer to contact, learn and file. How you use that tool of education to further your dreams, what you do with that tool or any tool, is what determines your future. Going to college doesn't guarantee anything. You alone are your best asset, to use the tools you develop in school, and mostly out of school, to the best of your ability. And you alone, no one else, can guarantee your own success.

Do you notice the emphasis I put on you and you alone? Too many people, I have met hundreds of them in my life time, always blame someone or something else for their failures and disappointments, which everyone who attempts anything has. They blame the weather, their father or mother, their boss, the wrong school, the country's economic situation, their bad back, the car broke down, you name it — but not themselves. They fail in life only because they cannot rise above their failures, whatever the reason, and learn something from them. They cannot square their shoulders, take a deep breath and move on.

You know about my own failure in not getting a free scholarship to Rutgers, my young years in the Air Force, my late start in life, my persistence and willingness to begin a new business with dad at the age of 58. All my three older brothers ever really gave me was a friendly pat on the back. My dad was foreign born and illiterate. It was all up to me, and I never gave up.

Neither did your dad. He started a new business, alone in his 50s, and he is working hard and smart and succeeding. He believes in his own abilities and in himself. Remember, Dad attended but didn't even graduate college, but he uses all the tools God gave him. He learns fast, adapts to new situations just as fast and works hard. It's all really very simple. Dad persists and never gives up.

One more important point: Could I really write letters like these to ordinary teenagers? You are my audience. You fully understand the ideas I am trying to convey to you, or else I wouldn't take the huge amount of time and effort it takes to write to you at all, being your grandpa or not. Grandma Myra and I know and love who you are as individuals. Understand that your intelligence and natural abilities only give you a jump start on life, not a guarantee.

You have to make full use of all your tools, those in your own head and even in someone else's head like your teachers, advisers, your dad, me and everyone else you meet. The world will never come to you. You have to go out meet the world. That effort begins for you right now, today. It serves no purpose to be bashful. Your dad and I talk to everybody. Talk to people, mingle with them, ask questions and listen; then get busy and do. You will persist, and you will reach your goals. Now get going on college.

Grandma Myra and I love you both very much,

Grandpa Gene

From Scott, on the Future

April 26, 2007

Grandma and Grandpa,

I really appreciate your concern for my future and your faith in me. Although I wouldn't expect anything less from family, it is comforting and reassuring to hear your interest expressed. It takes an immeasurable amount of character to lead and show us the path through life, especially without knowing exactly who we are or the situations we encounter as students in the 21st century. I don't mean to make you sound old and ignorant, because you are certainly not. I merely want to thank you and commend you on communicating your wisdom to us (Steven and me).

I am proud and honored to have such a grandfather who cares so much and actually acts on those feelings, and above all I am lucky. I am lucky to have such a great family and great genes. I love you and Grandma very much, and both of you have helped me become the person I am today. Just the examples you two have set for me are a guiding inspiration and help me understand what life is supposed to bring and how I should paddle my way through it. Thank you again; I hope to see you soon.

Love,
Scott

Assists to Swish, Advice for Scott

October 12, 2007

Dear Scott,

This is a very difficult letter for me to write. I thought about it a long time. Why a letter? It is because we rarely talk very much to each other about personal things. I have some heartfelt thoughts to say to you. In a few years, I may not be around to write or talk with you or communicate with you in any way. No one, except perhaps your dad or brothers, will give you as honest an assessment of their observations than I. They will have much more time with you so, I must make my own opportunities. Just remember that I love you very much and always wish you the best that life has to offer.

Let me give you some background. My father died when I was 29. He was foreign born, couldn't read or write and never quite assimilated into America. My brothers were much older than me, and never had much time for me in a personal way. They were busy building their own lives. I was essentially on my own. In order to stay out of the infantry, I took some college courses one summer to better qualify for enlistment into the Air Force. That was my decision, as was every subsequent decision for the rest of my life.

Here's what I am getting at. I played the hand I was dealt. Perhaps it was fortunate that I had to take charge of my life early. Each one of us must sooner or later direct and be responsible for his own life. Advice should always be sought from qualified people and all other sources. They provide a different perspective, ideas that may not have occurred to you. To enable you to make a more informed decision. It demonstrates not weakness but strength of purpose. Every president needs and seeks advice.

I know pretty well who you are. I know from your few wonderful letters to me; from our rare and brief conversations; your off-hand comments, often shrewd or funny, that I hear; and your visible kindnesses all tell me something about you. I remember vividly one comment you made to me about an election for governor at your mock political convention in Trenton. It was a shrewd assessment and well beyond your years. So I know my Scott, and I am extremely proud of you and who you are, as is Grandma Myra.

Life is much more than who you are. It's really what you do with who you are. A souped-up parked car just takes up space in the garage — a moving car has purpose. It is going somewhere. You have a basketball. You can either dribble in place indefinitely or shoot baskets. They may not all go in, but many will. Getting to college and many other journeys of life are the same thing, shooting baskets. After I asked you, "What's new?" you mentioned MIT. That is shooting at only one basket and suppose the ball doesn't go in. What about shooting other baskets, other colleges, that will give you just as good an education or better? The world doesn't begin and end with MIT. You mentioned early acceptance. Is your application in yet, or is it being prepared? Suppose it is rejected. Are you thinking of backups and many of them to hedge your bets? Remember this effort or lack of effort is for your future. Start shooting baskets today.

Have you talked to your father yet? What tuition can he afford? Remember he just started a new business. He also has Steven and Adam to think about. He's got many more financial responsibilities that you may not even be aware of. He pays your mother a large sum every month among many other demands on his resources. You should see where he stands and make an attempt to match your ambitions to his pocketbook. That is the prudent and the right thing to do. You want his money but not his counsel.

I can tell you from my long, active years and my association with thousands of successful people and many less successful, it's not where you go to college but how you apply yourself at college and after. There are hundreds of excellent schools, and degrees today are a dime a dozen. It is not the college. It's the man behind the degree that makes all the difference.

You also mentioned to me more than once how qualified you are both academically and extracurricular. I fully agree, and I admire your efforts and perseverance to become so qualified. However, at this point you are just a powerful parked car not going anywhere, and you are still dribbling.

I ask you a question about your quest for a college, and I get a pleasant but short answer, but no discussion, and no new ideas can emanate either from me or you if there is no discussion. I gave you a book about getting into college. That is the last I heard about it. Are you reading any of it, a little, a lot? Did you put it away, discuss some ideas it gave you with your dad? Maybe you threw it away.

Scott, living as a mental hermit within yourself and not talking definitively with your dad, or me or anyone else as far as

I know is a losing proposition. Open discussion with others, as I have practiced all my life, develops fresh ideas, helps formulate avenues of action, crystallizes ideas in your own mind, and saves many detours and failures for you later in your life. It also makes new friends and contacts. Two minds are better than one, and 10 are better than two. As you know, I talk to everybody. Why not? I am continually learning something new, meeting new people and opening new avenues of interest. It has worked beautifully for my 86 years to my everlasting benefit. I still practice it every day.

Your dad and I spoke to hundreds of people for advice and guidance for many months before we ever thought of or could even start Oak Tree. A stranger gave us the original idea. We liked it and jumped on it. We then talked to other office supply companies up for sale and milked their experience, to friends, strangers, possible suppliers, people who might know much more of what we were going to do than us. We distilled all this information and the wisdom of others and made our plans from a position of strength and knowledge. We saved time, money and possible failure, and we succeeded. It was no accident. I was 58, dad was 28, and we spoke to everybody. It works, and it's free. Our success is benefiting you today. Think about that.

My Scott, I love you and I only wish the best for you. I know you do not like gratuitous advice. But I cannot sit idly by and watch you wrestle with important decisions affecting your future welfare and not seek or benefit from the guidance and experience of others. Your time is now. Make the most of it now. I can't begin to tell you how fast 86 years flew by.

Grandpa Gene

Seasons of Motion

December 19, 2007

Hi Guys,

It's another season and another similar reason for being here. The weather is as advertised, warm, almost cool and clear. I have played golf each Monday, the last one wearing a jacket. We have frequented some of our favorite restaurants, and I have seen one movie. I exercise just about every day. Grandma Myra has returned to her games and woman stuff.

With all of this quiet life, I still would prefer to travel and be on the move to distant places. I am thinking about a trip to Alaska for 2008. With all this stuff about global warming, I should see the Arctic glaciers before they melt and become as extinct as the dinosaurs. We came around a little late for the latter. Maybe I should go to India and look up the Bengal tiger, another endangered species. However, the American Museum of Natural History may have a stuffed one, a far less dangerous proposition.

We all have our responsibilities. Mine now are to take care of Grandma Myra and keep myself in good shape. That is especially true and more difficult now when nature keeps reminding me, in various ways, that I have been around a long time. So far, I have taken care of that very easily by keeping my stride quick and active and the grass under my feet short.

You have your job to do, and just keep doing it well. Keep the grass short and keep moving. Grandma Myra and I love you both very much.

Grandpa Gene

Father's Day 2008, to Adam

June 21, 2008

Dear Adam,

Thank you for your wonderful Father's day card. And you signed it yourself! Soon you will be going to school and learning all about the world. It's a big world with a great deal to learn. But then you are only 4 and you have plenty of time. As you grow older, 5, then 6, 7 and 8, you will also learn to make good use of your time. You are 5, 6, 7 and 8 only once, and then you are all grown up. Listen always to your mother and dad and even your brothers, because they will be your closest and best friends all through your life.

We all love you very much.

Grandma Myra and Grandpa Gene

Real World and Self-Respect

March 4, 2009

Dear Adam, Steven and Scott,

I have always tried to close my letters to with a lesson for life, something you can take to the bank to ensure your happiness and prosperity. Success and happiness are personal to each of us. What applies to one may not be suitable to another. Do you like who you are? Are you pleased that you are doing the best you know how? Do you recognize and pursue the opportunities for personal growth that become available to you?

These are some of the questions you should be asking yourself as you enter the mainstream of society. You are confronted with choices all the time and must constantly decide which road to take. For instance, extracurricular activities can add to your well-being and personal development. Sharing experiences, doing things with others, broadens your horizons and cements relationships. Your school days are the most prolific friend-making time of your life. Many will last a lifetime.

There is yet another idea that few people ever think about. It involves a simple question that has no easy answer. How do you truly feel about yourself? Think about it. The answer is much more important to your future than how others feel about you. Too many people predicate their lives and efforts on pleasing others and end up fulfilling the wrong wish lists. Every one of us dances to a different drummer, and you must find your personal drum beat and develop it to suit your own individual dance.

There is a wise saying of unknown origin that the person who fools himself is the worst fool of all. Nothing propels a man towards his goals faster than an honest self-appraisal of who he really is, plus a never-ending effort to improve his skills and knowledge. Ask yourself these questions. Are you truly pleased with your work habits, your practicality of thought, your perseverance in the face of obstacles, your love of truth and your desire to excel in all your endeavors?

Always take personal pride and even joy in everything that you do. Self-respect is a continuous work in progress, and like wisdom, it can only be earned.

Grandma Myra and I love you very much,

Grandpa Gene

Everyone is a Friend

April 25, 2009

Dear Steven and Scott,

It was wonderful seeing you today. Grandma Myra and I are always available to see you when you have any free time. I will try my best not to lecture. I know it can be trying listening to stuff, much of which you already know. And then I tend to repeat myself. It can make for a trying time. My letters are pretty full of the same thoughts I talk about. Perhaps you can lecture me. Why not? You are bright, well-spoken and know quite a bit about this world at your young age. Remember, you see it from a different vantage point, and you certainly have valid and very worthy ideas.

Grandma and I are back in the New Jersey routine again. I am thinking ahead to a possible trip. I just hope Grandma remains stable. I was just out for a walk, and in a few weeks I go back to the gym. Exercise is good for me, indeed for everybody.

I seem to be so busy with photography, the computer, gym soon, lunches, poker and general reading. I just took four books out of the library that I asked the Roseland librarian to hold for me. By the way, she is my friend also. Everybody is my friend, because I show interest in the people I interact with, their problems, their employment and life challenges, and their basic well-being. Who else takes the time to care? But for me it lubricates the road of life, and the empathy I exhibit towards them, all of them, is greatly appreciated, and to be honest, reciprocated to my everlasting benefit. I love people. They are so human, foibles and all, and I learn so much.

Well fellows, take a moment to drop us a line. The effort will stretch your mind. After all, what can you say to your grandparents that they don't already know? Try it. Unload on us. My old shoulders are broad and can still carry a heavy load. Talk about anything at all — your life, your activities, even your problems. You have them like everyone else. Maybe from my point of view they would be simple to solve and may be not nearly so dire as they may seem to you right now. Remember the upside-down house — try a different perspective.

Your dad is going to be around long after us. Get to know him better. He's going through the same life experiences that we all do. Get his perspective. Talk to him more. He may surprise you.

Grandma and I love you very much and forever.

Grandpa Gene

Ask and Receive

November 17, 2009

Dear Steven and Scott,

Yesterday I was in my New Jersey bank, PNC, to get some
Christmas gift money. I needed different denominations. An
ATM, which I use only in New Jersey for free, only has 20s. As
I was leaving, I noticed one of the managers at his desk behind
a glass windowed office. I had talked to him once before, so he
knew who I was and my history with his bank. After the usual
pleasantries, I asked him if there was any way to use an ATM
that wasn't connected to his bank without a fee. He quickly said I
could, and he proceeded to arrange it right there.

Now no one had ever told me that before. I had to ask. Lesson
No. 1: I had always written a check for cash in Florida and then
went to Bank of America, my Florida bank, to cash it. I had to
keep a couple of CDs there in order for the privilege. There were
no PNC branches in Florida. But now I could use any ATM in
the world at no charge.

As a lark, I then asked him if PNC, my home bank, had any
branches in Florida. I had never seen any in all my years there.
He said that PNC very recently bought National City Bank with

1,200 branches countrywide and many branches in Florida. In fact, the signs in Florida were being changed this very week. He then went on a computer to print a list of the locations for me. I quickly noticed that there were two branches in Boynton Beach.

Now I can use the PNC Bank both in Florida and New Jersey and use ATMs worldwide, no charge. In one impromptu visit I learned two important facts that would make my overall banking experience much easier.

Lesson No. 2: Talk to people; they love to be noticed and recognized and are very often helpful. Make friends everywhere, even when you think you may not need them. Some day you may.

Love to you both,

Grandpa Gene

Creativity

March 11, 2010

Dear Scott,

I have been thinking of our conversation the other day, and I just want to record some ideas we discussed about the challenges of creativity.

First of all, be calm; don't force ideas, it can't be done. Ideas expose themselves like a sudden revelation. You know it when you see it. But what is the process that can foster ideas? What can one do to be creative?

From my own experience, here is what I have always done. Now these techniques are learned from writing my letters to you and your brothers, from years of being in and developing new business opportunities and from my years in advertising and marketing early in my career.

Ideas cannot be created in a vacuum. Assume I have a creative problem, and I have to develop new ways to expose it, to express it and to show it in order to foster a certain effect in the viewer or recipient. Try to answer these questions first. Who is my audience? What am I trying to say? What effect or result or reaction do I seek to get from them?

Then start with a piece of paper. Write down anything that comes to mind no matter how foolish, remote or irrelevant. Let your mind roam or even consciously hallucinate, turn it loose, imaginate (new word). You then begin to give your mind fodder upon which to feed and develop creative ideas. You can leave it for a while, or even a long while, and then come back to it. Your mind continues to work in the background, whatever else you do in the meantime.

Another way to generate mental fodder is to talk with someone, anyone at all, who will sincerely listen. It could be one individual or a group of two or more people. In my advertising days, we used to have four, five and six around the table ventilating mentally. You can also do this with someone on the phone as well. Explain to them your problem or purpose. They don't even have to understand your business or purpose. In their ignorance, they will ask foolish questions, make funny, irrelevant, stupid or even sage remarks, which may give you a whole new train of thought and even a new direction for you to pursue and think about. Your mind will then automatically begin to generate ideas of its own, many useful ideas, based on your knowledge, your expertise and training.

Other things you can do are take a walk, exercise, go for a drive, eat an apple, do something, but don't sit in a chair and just try to think. You must have confidence in yourself that you can be just as creative as anyone else. Don't be overwrought. It takes time, and it will all come together. It always does. Through all the confusion that may seem to be here now, be confident that it will work out. You and we know that you have the ability, and the rest is persistence and more persistence.

Please call me at any time, for any reason or no reason. If you have any questions on the above, call.

We love you,

Grandpa Gene

218 Think Clearly, Act Boldly

Think Clearly, Act Boldly

September 30, 2010

Dear Steven and Scott,

As you know, I had to cancel my trip to Europe due to illness. However, I always buy insurance. I faxed my claim for reimbursement to the insurance company last week. I felt that one week is enough to acknowledge receiving it. With email, and the fact that all my communications with them has been by email, I should have heard from them by now.

I called them this morning, Thursday, finally got a claim examiner on the phone and asked him to check my claim. After looking on the computer, he told me that he found it and would look it over and call me back in 20 minutes. I got his name and phone number and told him that I would be waiting for his call. I did tell him how nice it was to work with his company — how easy they made the insurance process, including the claim procedures.

He called me back in 20 minutes, said that he approved my claim and that I could expect payment early next week. I tried to pin him down as to exactly when and he offered by Tuesday.

Who knows how long it would have taken to settle my claim if I had not called? I know now that nothing was being done until I called. I also made sure that all the necessary papers were in the claim and that they had everything they needed so as not to delay my payment. That included medical records; doctor's report and letter; and airline and cruise line charges and receipts.

Also, and this is very important, they record every call. Make sure you say nothing that could in any way jeopardize your claim. He did ask questions, and I answered very blandly. He asked me if I have booked another trip and I said, "no." How do I feel? "Not yet back to normal." Some people talk too much. Well, you get the message. Think clearly, act boldly.

I love you both,

Grandpa Gene

Peace and Quiet

December 13, 2010

Dear Steven and Scott,

Grandma Myra and I are here in Florida over a week and pretty well settled in. It's been quite cold, especially today starting out in the 40s. It is not what we came here for, but is still better than New Jersey. Similar temperatures seem colder in Florida than in New Jersey, even to northerners.

Grandma Myra and I are looking forward to your visits. It may not be exciting for you, but it is a break and a change of pace. Years from now, when you look back on your visits to your grandparents in Florida, you may remember them solely for their non-demanding peace and quiet in a hectic world.

The only continuous excitement for me is traveling. Even in the Air Force, when they put me on orders to move somewhere else, I was thrilled, even to be going overseas to the Philippine Islands. Maybe, like you, I get bored easily unless I'm doing something — reading, exercising, conversing, computing or even thinking through a problem.

Please remember, learn something new every day.

Grandma and I love you both,

Grandpa Gene

Lake Placid

September 6, 2011

Dear Raellen and Billy,

I slept little last night thinking about your interest in a Lake Placid home. When you get through reading this email, you will get a good idea about how I feel.

Assuming you're able to buy this place cheap, say for $100,000 to $150,000, put in another $100,000 to $150,000, giving you a cost basis of about $300,000. There are, however, other more important considerations than cost. How often will you go there? How long will you stay — a total of a month a year, two months, three months? Will you go up one weekend a month, two a month, even three? Remember, you already own a beautiful home, surrounded by trees, with a pool on a high-rise overlooking a private lake on four acres of forested land and very close to civilization.

What will you do when you get there? Swim? Where? Hike? Go out with friends? What friends? Eat out, drive around, go sightseeing, chop wood? You will still have to do laundry, go shopping for food, clean the place every time you enter it, wash dishes, prepare a meal and maintain it in every respect. You do all of that now, and you don't have to drive 10 hours' roundtrip to throw out uneaten food, drain the pipes and heat the place in winter whether you are there or not. Maintenance on any house is never ending and especially a mostly empty house where issues unnoticed can get worse before you find it.

Let's talk about renovation. You are doing a reconstruction in Andover. You are looking for contractors, trying to find someone you can trust, and you are here to check his progress and monitor results against his requests for payments. Remember the problems you had building your house, or two houses? You know the troubles better than anybody. A contractor is a contractor whether in New Jersey or Lake Placid. He calls you on the phone, "Mr. Kesselman, I finished phase one, and I need another $10,000 to continue the job." How many times will you have to drive there to check their work and keep them honest, if one ever can? That kind of aggravation you don't need. That renovation in Lake Placid will take over your whole life and suck you dry.

Let's talk about Adam. He is 7 now, soon 8, 9, 10 and more. As he gets older, which happens quickly, will he want to leave his friends and familiar surroundings and traipse off with his parents to a boring time (for him) in Lake Placid? Of course, your mother is close, but you cannot depend on her to be an on-call babysitter every time you come up, unless she becomes a permanent visiting resident. Adam needs his friends, not old people, to help him mature, get along with his peers and develop his personality.

When will you go there? Spring, summer, fall? But you want to travel, go places, see the world. Where will you get the time to do all that? The house in Lake Placid will become a ball and chain around your neck. What do you do first, go to Lake Placid because you own it and it's costing a fortune, or take a luxurious cruise around the Hawaiian Islands? It's a big world, and there's a lot to see, places to visit and scenery you cannot imagine. You do not have the time to do everything.

Let's talk cost. For argument's sake, the house costs $300,000 if we're lucky. We are not finished yet. The moment you file for construction permits, your taxes start to rise. They could double or more with all the additions and changes you would have to make. There is home insurance, utilities that you cannot shut on and off, because you want them when you go up and continual heat in winter. You can't leave the house to the elements. There is the cost of a caretaker to look the place over when you are not around. With normal maintenance the annual upkeep could touch a minimum of $25,000 to $35,000 per year.

You keep the house 10 years, for argument's sake. You have tied up $300,000 that is not producing an extra penny for you — that is nonperforming.

Suppose the money would earn 5 percent; it could be less or much more. That $15,000 not earned would be added to the cost of your overhead, and now the annual upkeep starts approaching $50,000. If you spent four weeks a year there, your weekly cost, not counting the ride up and all the housekeeping chores you would perform, would cost you $12,000 per week. Eight weeks, would cost you $6,000 per week. That's one hell of a vacation in the same old place all the time.

You can take issue with these figures, but you cannot argue with this logic. It would be far cheaper to go to Whiteface Lodge or any luxurious hotel in the entire world than stay even one day at this forest hideout.

You would be free as the air, see the world on your own time, pay for your visit and go home refreshed. You would be ready to enjoy your beautiful home in the mountains with a swimming pool, situated on a high knoll overlooking a tranquil lake and surrounded by virgin forest where you and Adam have many friends and an active social life. It's your anchor.

You want to get away? Plan a trip, anywhere, for an hour, a day, five days, a week, two weeks, pay for it once and have a ball.

Love,
Dad

Change and Support

January 2, 2012

Dear Billy and Raellen, Adam, Steven, and Scott,

Yes, even I cannot find the words to express how I truly feel
about your total support during this worst time of my life. No
family on earth could have done any more to get a parent and
grandparent through this terrible period. Sixty-eight years
of marriage, almost 90 years of life, vanished in an instant — just
like a magician's trick. Only this trick cannot be undone or even
explained logically. It must be accepted, and you are helping me
to accept it.

You did what had to be done immediately with no prior
preparation or forethought, and your numerous kindnesses will
remain in my heart forever. Whatever Myra was, she was my wife
and your mother and grandmother. Whatever she did, she always
did the best she could and did it the only way she knew how.
Thank you, thank you and thank you for being who you are and
for being my family.

I love each of you very much,

Dad (Grandpa)

Problem Account

March 1, 2012

Dear Billy,

There nothing more for you to say to get that account back. They know your story, and they have a long history with you. Any more sales talk from you would seem like desperation.

The trick is to get them to talk. You must hear from them, put them on the spot and get their take on the situation. They stopped buying, you didn't stop selling. Therefore, they have to talk to you and get off their chest whatever is bothering them.

You must ask them directly what their problem is, why they stopped buying, quickly, with no explanation as to why you are asking. Ask a polite, quick question on your part, short and fast, and then be still. Let the moment stay silent as long as it takes them to answer. Put them on the spot. It worked for me a hundred times. Try it.

Love,
Dad

Sticking Your Neck Out

March 12, 2012

Dear Billy, Raellen, Adam, Scott and Steven,

Your visit to Florida was a real joy. I enjoyed every minute you were here, even when you went to Miami because you were coming back after the game. Golf was wonderful also, and we had a great time and in beautiful weather.

My new TV set is a pleasure to watch. In fact, I watched my first movie on it, while you were here Sunday night, on HBO. Thank you, all of you, Billy, Raellen, Adam, Scott and Steven. It's a birthday present that will keep on giving me joy.

Now it's quiet here, and I have been busy on trying to make appointments to keep busy over the next week or two. Some people I like and some I don't, but it beats staying home alone. I am trying to build some kind of routine, and I will have to do that in New Jersey when I return home. I am making my lists now, pulling in names from out of my past.

It's like a business, getting customers and building accounts. To get anywhere in this life, I learned early you have to stick your neck out like a turtle. He can't move a muscle until his head comes out of its shell.

I love all of you very much, you are my family and you are all I have.

Grandpa Gene

Making the Most of Your Life

May 28, 2012

Dear Adam, Steven and Scott,

In medieval times, a quest was a chivalrous journey in search of romance and adventure. It was a noble undertaking by knights errant, marked by honor, generosity, courtesy, to seek the favor of the opposite sex and to protect the weak. Most people in those years struggled just to survive, much less embark on a quest for fame and fortune. They often lived their whole lives within a few hundred yards of where they were born.

Our world has changed greatly in a 1,000 years. Yet, one fact and one fact alone continues to be true over all these long years: People themselves never change. Throughout the millennia, the same hungers and needs that motivate all peoples everywhere are still present today in each of us. Then, as well as now, we all wanted love, understanding, recognition, appreciation, approval, happiness and everything else that would seem to make our lives worth living. How each of us achieve any of the above similarities during our lives then becomes the true measure of our personal and individual differences.

Today, in this fast-moving 21st century, we are still knights
errant on our own personal quests. We still want romance and
adventure and all the comforts and privileges of life. We have the
entire world and almost all its knowledge right at our fingertips.
We can travel afar over land, sea and in the air the world over
in hours. Have 1,000 years made it any easier for us to make the
most of our lives?

The answer as ever before, and as it will always be, lies within
each of you. It has nothing to do with the times in which you
live, then or now. It has everything to do with you personally,
who you are as an individual, your talents, your motivations, your
ambitions, and your emotional and physical well-being. Simply
put, making the most of your life is making the most of who you
are.

Knowing who you are implies knowing what you are good
at — your basic abilities, your talents. It also includes doing
what you enjoy, a vocation that gives you satisfaction and joy
and a wonderful feeling of accomplishment. When you seek a
life of doing what you are good at and what you enjoy, then your
opportunity for success and happiness is limitless. The problem is
that many of us never seem to know well enough exactly what we
want or what our true abilities are. We often pursue goals with
full sincerity, commitment and belief, without proper thought as
to who we are.

Therefore, finding yourself early in life is the true measure
of your growing maturity. Therein lies the simplest answer to
your future happiness and your total well-being as an individual.
If you can learn who you truly are as a human being, you will be
better able to narrow your choices and prevent false starts and

unrealistic goals. It will allow you to determine more precisely where you belong in life. You will then be working within your God-given capabilities and thereby find it vastly easier to fulfill your hopes and dreams.

I love each of you very much,

Grandpa Gene

Think!

November 18, 2012

Dear Adam, Steven and Scott,

You and I both know people who in varying degrees see but don't observe, listen but don't hear and think but don't understand. Their reality is self-centered, and they act as if the world operates only on their set of rules. They are frequently quite difficult to talk to and reason with, especially if the ideas you express did not originate with them. Their thinking is often contrary, and their minds seem to be myopic much of the time. Let us look at some of these people.

He drives 60 miles an hour in a driving rainstorm with the visibility under 10 feet. He is late for an appointment and offers no excuse or apology. He drinks you under the table and doesn't offer to pay for his excesses. In a discussion or a difference of opinion he sees no merit at all in your side, and no compromise for your point of view. He will often argue unreasonably for a tenuous or untenable position. In general, he sees, hears and thinks in a sterile atmosphere, and his mind is blind to much of the truth that surrounds him on all sides. He lives only in the reality of his own world.

The above descriptions are not absolute but will be manifest in many people from time to time. I am now talking about a small businessman who loves to sell and talk to people. At the same time, he makes a minimum effort in collecting money due him on sales. In six months he is out of money and out of business and wonders why. He thinks his customers just didn't pay him what they owe. He doesn't recognize his own neglect of a major business function. After all, look how fast his sales were expanding.

I am talking about a man who opens a restaurant with good food and a comfortable atmosphere. After the usual initial splurge his tables are soon empty. The parking area is not sufficient or configured properly for all the businesses that occupy his location. He just didn't see the obvious, which should have been evident even before he rented the space.

I am talking about any activity, business or personal, where the execution may be one sided and does not cover all the factors required for success or approval. If you run a business, your entire operation must be monitored concurrently. That means sales, accounting, customer service, product quality and pricing, purchasing, employee training and performance, cost containment, efficiency of procedures, planning, and growth. Should you neglect any one facet of a business, its future can be in jeopardy.

In a smaller vein, you are dressing for an occasion. All parts of your grooming must be proper. Wear shoes that are shined, see that your hair is cut, and that your colors match and so forth. Be complete in all your activities, whatever it turns out to be. As in baseball, you must try to cover all your bases. Good players can field, hit, run and throw. Good golfers must be able to drive, chip and putt. All good athletes practice constantly to keep their entire game sharp. They take nothing for granted.

I have often wondered why many people are so blind or even indifferent to the realities and the truths that stare them right in the face. Is it because they lack a basic curiosity or plain common sense? Can it be arrogance or insecurity? Are they greedy, selfish, self-centered, overly competitive, excessively egotistic, impatient or have a host of other characteristics? It really doesn't matter. The results are the same and most often less than satisfactory.

Resolve in your mind right now to always try to do the right thing. Be totally complete in your endeavors and resolve to cover all your bases. It means thinking about problems and situations from every possible angle — left to right, front to back and top down. And take your sweet time doing it, either overnight, or as many days as it takes. Then be definitive and make a decision. It may not turn out to be the best, or the most satisfactory, but you took the time to think it through. Simplify your world. Clean up your mental desk. Make decisions and keep moving ahead. Do not clutter your brains with unresolved problems. Calm your own seas, then move on and live your lives.

Love you,

Grandpa Gene

Luck

January 24, 2013

Dear Adam, Steven and Scott

How lucky I am to live this long and be allowed to see my two older grandsons maturing into manhood and the youngest exhibiting his intelligence early in life? I am very proud of each of you.

Steven and Scott, your visits to me in Florida were extremely joyful. We did fun things together and talked more than with any other visit. You seem to be easier, more open and friendlier with people. Keep developing that wonderful personality trait. It makes life and living so much more pleasant and satisfying.

You both had the patience to teach me a whole new email address on a brand new computer. Whenever I called for help, which was frequent, you were there without delay. Steven was on call for the last days of the old computer. I learned a lot from both you and also learned a lot about you in the process.

Steven and Scott, you have the ability to take on the world. As I did at your age, take steps now to overcome any psychological and emotional roadblocks that could stand in the way of your assured success. A clean engine always works better. There is

help available. Use it. Talk to people as I do. Be confident. Just
know you have what it takes. Go for it and persevere. No one will
ever ask where you are coming from or about your growing up
problems They only see you as you are today. Change what you
must. Just do it.

God bless all of you.

Love,
Grandpa Gene

Constant Motion, From Scott

January 25, 2013

Grandpa,

I had a wonderful time with you in Florida. Thank you so much for everything. We enjoyed some new settings and had a great time at some old standbys. Going to the Banana Boat with you will never get old. Every day, the sky has different features to show us, the water moves in a slightly different way, new boats sail by our view, and new and unique people are around us every time. I even got to try several new dishes, each as well prepared as the last and always paired with what we have come to conclude may be the best soup in the world.

I'm so glad you are trying to make the most of your new computer and email address. Most people would be discouraged by the number of processes you are learning with the nuances of Gmail and your new computer.

It is very cold here, and it has taken some adjusting getting bundled up after eight days of the mild Florida air. Despite the cold, I have been attacking each day head on, feeding my body and my mind well, and working hard towards my goals.

You have always been an incredible grandfather to Steven, Adam and me, and we are growing closer as friends. Few people get to have such a strong relationship with their grandparents, and I am grateful we have gotten to know each other.

Keep moving.

I love you,

Scott

Balance

January 28, 2013

Dear Scott,

Great note. You are beginning to notice the beautiful world around you and the people in it. Talk to them; it is very rewarding and healthy. You are developing a positive attitude, a can-do attitude and a goal of doing something creative and positive every day. You are greasing the skids and tuning the machine that will eventually make your high intelligence pay off. I am proud of you.

All this takes lots of energy, so don't spend it all on exercise. Thirty to 40 minutes a day is plenty. You need high energy levels to fuel brain power to think, to do, to create and to be productive. A constantly tired or aching body is not conducive to creative performance. Also, try not to be too obsessed with your physical well-being or your food mix. All I did was sensible eating and moderate exercise, and I made it so far to 91 plus. I never knew what an ab was until recently.

Some philosopher once said that a balanced life is true moderation in all things. May I suggest that you rethink some of your daily priorities? I say that because before this, you had fewer productive goals and had more time to kill and think and spend time on your physical well-being. Now that you are spending more creative time on your future, your daily schedule must be reoriented, and more organized and formal. Don't over worry anymore about your body, your abs, protein, stretching, joints, and on and on. Your life will still continue in good health. You have other worthwhile goals to occupy most of your time now.

Call me or your Dad at any time to discuss these subjects.

Love,
Grandpa

Grief and Company

March 12, 2013

Dear Scott,

It is never easy to lose a friend at any age. I have lost almost all my old friends, and it doesn't get any easier even at my age. However, life has taught me something. I have learned to roll with the punches and move on. There is really no other choice. The family I grew up with is all gone — my wife of 68 years, cousins, hundreds of acquaintances and even those that have briefly touched me on my long journey. My world has turned over many times, and every time I have moved on with all the wonderful memories tucked somewhere back in my mind out of the way.

Grief is always personal, but remember you have obligations to yourself to go ahead with your life. Honor your friend's life by persisting with your own and making your own dreams come true. If you persist with your job and toward your goals, I know your play will work out, your life will work out, and you will definitely be successful and happy. Always keep moving, always. Life is good.

Let me remind you, Scott, you are not alone in this world. You have family. They are a major part of your assets at your age. Have you ever thought about the experience your father has in persisting throughout his life? He has overcome many major problems, more than his share, and look what he has accomplished. And there is Steven, your own brother and contemporary. Take them into your confidence. Have conversations with them, talk to them, bounce your ideas and problems and concerns off their own unique points of view — over dinner, over the phone, in the car. Your own "backyard" can be a cornucopia of new and exciting directions of thought. Remember what I once wrote you about being creative and talking to others for ideas. Go ahead and talk to them.

Love,
Grandpa

Gene Kesselman was born and raised in Newark, New Jersey, graduating from Weequahic High School in 1939. During World War II he served in the Air Force as an aerial navigator on a B-24 bomber and later at the headquarters of Pacific Air Command at Fort McKinley, Manila, earning the rank of 1st Lieutenant. Upon returning from the war, he resumed his education and graduated from Rutgers University School of Business with a Bachelor of Science in Marketing. For many years he taught business and marketing at Rutgers, then became a successful independent sales rep before eventually going into business with his son Bill.

At the age of 80, Gene began writing email letters to his grandchildren, Scott, Steven and soon Adam. Over the next 15 years, his use of email connected his family and enabled his grandchildren to not only see their grandfather as a friend, but also to better understand themselves and the world around them in the process. This book is the complete collection of these letters.